THE
CURRABINNY
COOKBOOK

THE

CURRABINNY COOKBOOK

JAMES KAVANAGH
&
WILLIAM MURRAY

PHOTOGRAPHY BY
BRÍD O'DONOVAN

PENGUIN
IRELAND

TO THE MEMORY

OF

JENNY MURRAY, 1987–2007

CONTENTS

INTRODUCTION

'All sorrows are less with bread'
Miguel de Cervantes

Welcome to *The Currabinny Cookbook*!

For us, food is life's greatest pleasure, so it has been a labour of love to bring together recipes to answer that simplest of questions, *What do I want to eat?*

This question will arise in all kinds of environments and moods, whether you're living in the city or the countryside, getting home late from a long day's work and using mainly store-cupboard ingredients to make something simple, or – with the luxury of time – shopping for fresh produce and preparing ingredients for a more complicated recipe. Whatever your circumstances, we believe your food should taste great and be a source of enjoyment and comfort.

But first, who are we?

Well, we're not chefs or any kind of experts. We're just devoted foodies and home cooks. Both of us grew up in homes – William in Currabinny on Cork Harbour, James in Rathfarnham in South Dublin – where delicious, freshly prepared meals and baking were par for the course (thanks, Breda and Gags!).

After completing his Fine Art degree, William decided to explore his passion for cooking by doing the three-month course at the legendary Ballymaloe Cookery School. At the same time, James was working in public relations and two of the clients he worked with were iconic Irish brands, Barry's Tea and Kerrygold Butter. Having to think about what made these brands great – quality and tradition – sowed a seed in James that came to fruition when we got together.

Our shared obsession with great food and cooking made us realize that it was more than just an interest – it was something we wanted to make our life's work.

After spending a summer in Currabinny, talking and dreaming about selling our food at markets, catering, doing pop-up food events, one day owning a café, writing a cookbook, we started brainstorming names for our baby. And of course the perfect name was staring us in the face ...

Currabinny is a peninsula that projects into Cork Harbour between the port of Ringaskiddy and the fishing and sailing village of Crosshaven. Currabinny Woods rise steeply behind houses that are strung along the water's edge, looking across to Crosshaven. It's a quiet and picturesque place, dominated by trees, rocks and water.

In Currabinny there is a huge interest in food. While there is a respect for tradition, and families have their own recipes that have been handed down from one generation to the next, there is also an appetite for experimentation and innovation. People are in the habit of foraging for ingredients from both land and sea. Recipes, techniques and new discoveries are generously shared between neighbours. (Indeed, on page 213 local botanical artist Patrick O'Hara shares his wonderful elderflower cordial recipe.)

Fishing and tending a small vegetable patch are both second nature to William. And inspired by his mother, he grew up experimenting with and inventing ways to use the produce that came from outside the kitchen window.

So Currabinny is not just a place we love, but the food culture there embodies everything we admire and value as an approach to cooking and eating – drawing on the best of local produce and old traditions while being willing to try new things.

For us, cooking is about curiosity, community and, above all else, taste. We tend to toggle between countryside and city, taking things we've seen and learned in Dublin to Cork to tease out and develop – and vice versa.

CURRABINNY IS NOT JUST A PLACE WE LOVE, BUT THE FOOD CULTURE THERE EMBODIES EVERYTHING WE ADMIRE

When we're in the city, nothing pleases us more than exploring cafés and restaurants, seeing classics done brilliantly or reinvented, and also getting a feel for emerging flavours and innovative methods of cooking.

And when we're in Currabinny, we will while away a day sailing around Cork Harbour, pulling into new places and trying out whatever is on offer. You'll find us picking samphire along the shore, buying vegetables at a farmers' market and some fish or meat from a fishmonger or butcher, and then discussing what we're going to make for dinner all the way home.

We love the fact that when we're in Cork we have uninterrupted time to develop our food ideas and come up with recipes that we can refine further in Dublin, where things are a little faster paced for us. This call-and-response pattern is something that has arisen naturally out of our lifestyle, but it has been a crucial influence on the evolution of Currabinny as a company and has shaped our food vision.

WE LIKE TO BE SPONTANEOUS AND FRESH AND WE ALSO LIKE TO MAKE OLD FAVOURITES AGAIN AND AGAIN WITH CONTEMPORARY, BOLD TWISTS

In our cooking we like to be spontaneous and fresh and we also like to make old favourites again and again with contemporary, bold twists. We have made all kinds of food; some dishes have been resounding successes and others not so much.

By taking the time to experiment, to be curious and to take risks, to do it the wrong way and then correct course, adding a little more of this or less of that, we have developed a repertoire of recipes that we love and that we know that other people love too. For us, this is the essence of cooking and enjoying food: trying out things, refining recipes until they are truly delicious, sharing.

As we said, we're not experts. We don't so much have rules as guiding principles. We believe in making an effort to source ingredients locally and to support small producers. And we like to eat seasonably and sustainably.

We have no interest in advising people on their diets and what to eat. Of course, we strongly believe in a varied diet and a healthy attitude to eating, but we don't demonize any ingredients, especially when they might be simply misunderstood.

We stand for balance, but not sacrifice. Food is about pleasure – eat well and not just to survive. There are no villains in these pages, only heroes.

....

WE DON'T DEMONIZE ANY INGREDIENTS

....

Some ingredients you will see popping up repeatedly because they are the bedrock of our cooking. For instance, butter. Butter got quite a hammering in the past due to the fierce marketing of manufactured 'spreads'. But butter is back – and we're delighted. We strongly believe in butter, and why wouldn't we when Ireland produces the best and richest butter in the world?

Use butter sensibly, of course, but remind yourself that it is completely natural and full of good fats and nutrients. (Where we include butter we mean regular salted butter; we sometimes reduce the amount of salt in a recipe to compensate. And of course all our dairy ingredients are full fat!)

Something that might seem a world away from butter and more conventional ingredients is seaweed, something we also love to cook with. But seaweed could be as ordinary an ingredient in the Irish kitchen as it is in the Japanese. Not only that, but Irish seaweed is softer, more palatable and less mass produced than other versions. It is also incredibly good for you and a natural sustainable product. You won't be surprised to hear that we have a recipe for a seaweed butter!

We cover all the bases – breakfast and brunch, breads, soups, salads, meat, fish, vegetable and pasta-based mains, side dishes, sweet things.* Something we think is a little unique is our chapter on preserves, condiments and dips. We have tons of recipes for these and have shared a selection of them here. They are all delicious in their own right for simple snacking, but we also use them lavishly in our cooking to enhance other dishes, so you'll see them cross-referenced through the book.

....

WE HOPE THE RECIPES IN THESE PAGES WILL NOURISH, COMFORT AND DELIGHT YOU AS MUCH AS THEY HAVE US!

....

Finally, anyone who knows us – or is aware of us via social media – knows how much we like to create a sense of occasion. So with that in mind we have shared our thoughts on how to set the scene for a truly special dinner.

Please leaf through, get hungry, get excited, experiment. We hope the recipes in these pages will nourish, comfort and delight you as much as they have us!

*Temperatures are for fan ovens. If you're using a conventional oven, please increase the temperature given by 20 degrees.

BREAKFAST & BRUNCH

Poached Eggs Three Ways

Waking up on a cold morning to find two glass bottles of milk and half a dozen fresh eggs delivered to the door is something that we think should be revived – for the good of the nation. Have one of these poached egg recipes with lots of buttery toast for breakfast and you'll be set up for the day!

SERVES 1

· 2 very fresh organic eggs

· white vinegar

· sea salt and freshly ground
  black pepper

METHOD

Make sure you use really good-quality eggs. Bring a medium-sized saucepan of water to a simmer and add a few dashes of white vinegar.

We find it best to crack the eggs first into a small cup or bowl. Create a whirlpool in the water with a spoon, then slowly tip in the eggs one at a time. Cook for around 3 minutes.

Remove the eggs on to kitchen paper using a slotted spoon, then transfer to a warmed plate. Cut away any scraggly bits of egg, and season lightly with salt and pepper.

They are perfect just like this, with some sourdough toast, but here are three of our favourite ways to enhance them.

PROSCIUTTO, PRESERVED LEMON CREAM AND PARSLEY

- 4 thin slices of prosciutto
- around 150ml preserved lemon and thyme cream (see page 80)
- 1 tablespoon chopped fresh flat-leaf parsley leaves

Get a warm plate ready. Place the prosciutto in a hot frying pan and cook for a few seconds until it crisps up.

In a small saucepan, gently heat the preserved lemon and thyme cream and drizzle it over the warm plate using a large spoon. Place the crispy prosciutto in the middle, your poached eggs on top, and sprinkle everything with parsley.

Or, again, you could serve the lot on buttery toast – eggs, prosciutto, and then the lemon cream as a dressing.

BLACK PUDDING AND MUSHROOM À LA CRÈME

- 2 large slices of good-quality black pudding, such as O'Herlihy's or Rosscarbery
- mushroom à la crème (see page 155 – use the full quantity from that recipe)

Get a warm plate ready. Place the black pudding slices under a hot grill for around 10 minutes, turning once. Place them on the warm plate, put your poached eggs on top and pour the mushroom à la crème over everything.

This is great in the winter when it is cold outside and you need something to stick to your bones!

Continued on page 27

- 4–6 spring onions
- olive oil
- 1 slice of toasted sourdough, buttered
- spring onion vinaigrette (see page 177)
- a few fresh flat-leaf parsley leaves, chopped

SEARED SPRING ONIONS AND SPRING ONION VINAIGRETTE

Trim and cut the spring onions lengthways. Put a griddle or grill pan on a high heat, place the spring onions into the pan and drizzle with a little olive oil. Cook until wilted and lightly charred.

Drape over buttered sourdough, place your poached eggs on top and drizzle generously with the zingy spring onion vinaigrette, finishing with some parsley. By far our favourite way to have poached eggs.

Kippers with Kombu Butter and Toast

Most mornings William's grandmother made smoked kippers, fried with a little butter, for his grandad. So this recipe is in memory of them. We love them with a nice bit of cider and honey loaf, toasted and spread generously with some salty, smoky kombu butter.

SERVES 1

- 1 tablespoon olive or rapeseed oil
- 2 smoked kippers
- 2 thick slices of tasty bread, such as Irish cider and honey loaf (see page 50)
- 100g kombu butter (see page 173)
- ½ a lemon, for squeezing
- sea salt and freshly ground black pepper
- 1 tablespoon chopped fresh flat-leaf parsley leaves

METHOD

In a large frying pan, heat the oil over a medium flame. Add the kippers and cook for 2 to 5 minutes per side.

Toast the bread until golden. Smother the slices with the kombu butter and arrange on a plate, placing the kippers on top. Squeeze some lemon juice over the kippers and season with salt, pepper and the chopped parsley.

Macroom Oatmeal with Milk and Salt

You will see Macroom Oatmeal mentioned more than once in this book – and not just because it's from Co. Cork! It's because it's the king of oatmeal. It's wonderful on its own with a pinch of salt or with some fruit and honey. Use whatever fruit is good, ripe and in season. In winter, homemade jam is a perfect addition to porridge.

SERVES 1–2

- 1 teacup of water
- 1½ teacups of milk
- a good pinch of sea salt
- ½ teacup of Macroom Oatmeal
- soft brown sugar (optional)

METHOD

Put all the ingredients except the sugar into a saucepan on a medium heat and stir continuously. The oats will absorb the liquid very fast, so be careful not to let the mixture stick to the bottom.

After about 5 or 6 minutes, when the oatmeal has softened and is at the consistency of porridge, transfer to a bowl and sprinkle with a little bit of brown sugar if desired.

WITH SATURN PEACHES, POMEGRANATE AND RAW HONEY

Follow the same recipe as above, but use just a **tiny pinch of sea salt**. When you have transferred the oatmeal to your bowl, arrange **some slices of good ripe Saturn peaches** (also called doughnut peaches) in the middle, sprinkle **a few pomegranate seeds** over and drizzle generously with **good-quality raw honey**. Orange blossom or wildflower varieties work really well.

Rye Spring Onion Pancakes with Lime and Chilli Butter

These pancakes are extremely healthy but still packed with flavour. The rye flour really complements the spinach and spring onion, and is full of fibre and lower in gluten than regular flour. Especially good when paired with the zingy lime and chilli butter!

SERVES 2

FOR THE LIME AND CHILLI BUTTER:

- 1 small clove of garlic
- a handful of fresh coriander leaves
- 2½cm piece of fresh red chilli
- juice of 1 lime
- a pinch of sea salt
- 100g butter, softened

FOR THE PANCAKES:

- 8 spring onions
- a handful of fresh chives
- 200g fresh baby spinach
- 100g rye flour
- 2 tablespoons baking powder
- 2 medium organic eggs
- 50g butter, melted
- 1 teaspoon ground coriander
- 75ml milk
- sea salt and freshly ground black pepper
- 1 tablespoon rapeseed oil, for frying

METHOD

First prepare the lime and chilli butter. Peel and crush the garlic, chop the coriander and finely dice the chilli. Put these into a bowl with the lime juice, salt and butter, and mash together with a fork or wooden spoon. When well combined, roll the butter into a log shape, wrap in baking parchment and cool in the fridge.

Finely slice the spring onions and chop the chives. Cook the baby spinach with a splash of water in a small pan until completely wilted. Drain and squeeze excess water out by pressing into wads of kitchen paper. Chop the spinach and put into a large bowl with the rest of the pancake ingredients, apart from the rapeseed oil. Mix well with a wooden spoon.

Put the oil into a frying pan on a medium-high heat. When hot, drop ladlefuls of the mixture into the pan – you should be able to cook 3 pancakes at a time. Cook each side for around 3 minutes until golden. Serve each pancake with a round of lime and chilli butter (cut from the roll and parchment removed) melting on top.

Buckwheat Pancakes

Our neighbour Naomi gave us this recipe, which comes all the way from New Zealand. The combination of nutty buckwheat – full of vitamins and protein – along with the probiotics in the yoghurt makes for an amazing start to the day.

SERVES 2

· 100g buckwheat flour
· 1 tablespoon caster sugar
· a pinch of sea salt
· 250ml milk
· 1 tablespoon natural yoghurt
· 1 medium organic egg
· 125ml water
· butter and rapeseed oil, for frying

METHOD

Whisk the flour, sugar, salt, milk, yoghurt and egg together in a large mixing jug. Slowly whisk in all the water, until the batter is smooth and runny.

Put a saucepan of water on to simmer and get a plate that will fit comfortably over the top.

Place a large frying pan over a high heat, melt a tablespoon of butter and a little rapeseed oil in it and lower the heat to medium. Pour in the batter to the size you want your pancake to be and cook until the underside is golden, then flip it over and cook the other side.

The whole process should take only around 2 minutes, a minute on each side. Repeat with the rest of the batter.

As you cook them, stack your pancakes on the plate placed over the simmering water. Serve with lemon juice, sugar, golden or maple syrup, Nutella, jam or butter.

Blueberry Buttermilk Drop Scones

'Go on, invite them down.' Ten minutes later the sliding door in the kitchen in Currabinny would be pulled back and four or five kids would march in, chattering away about what time the tide would be in for swimming. And soon the warm smell of the drop scones would fill the kitchen. It's a ritual that continues to this day when we're visiting Currabinny!

SERVES 4

- 75g cream flour
- 500ml buttermilk
- 2 teaspoons caster sugar
- 1 teaspoon bicarbonate of soda
- 1 medium organic egg
- 1 tablespoon butter, melted
- 80g fresh blueberries
- milk, for thinning the batter (optional)
- butter and rapeseed oil, for frying

METHOD

In a large mixing bowl, whisk the flour and buttermilk together with the sugar, bicarbonate of soda, egg and melted butter. Stir in the blueberries and leave the mixture to stand for at least 30 minutes.

The mixture should be the consistency of thick syrup when you come to cook the scones. If the mixture is too thick, add a little milk to thin it out again. Put a saucepan of water on to simmer and get a plate that will fit comfortably over the top.

Place a frying pan over a high heat, melt some butter and a little rapeseed oil in it and lower the heat to medium. Using a tablespoon as your measure, drop a spoonful of the batter on to the pan – there might be room to cook 2 or 3 at a time, depending on the size of your pan. Let the drop scones cook for 1 to 2 minutes on each side until golden brown all over.

Pile batches of your scones on to the plate placed over the simmering water until all of them are done. Drop scones should be served when everyone is sitting around the table, with freshly squeezed orange juice and a choice of black coffee or Barry's Tea.

Maple or golden syrup, lemon juice and even a little butter are all acceptable options with which to adorn your drop scones.

BREAD

Irish Stout and Treacle Loaf

Is there anything better than rich, salty Irish butter spread generously on a slice of nutty homemade bread? We think it's an irresistible combination, and this brown bread – dense and slightly sweet and malty – is the perfect companion to butter, though it's delicious on its own too.

MAKES 10 SLICES

- Butter for greasing
- 200g strong white flour
- 375g Macroom Stoneground Wholewheat Flour (extra coarse)
- 1 teaspoon bicarbonate of soda
- 1½ teaspoons sea salt
- 50g rolled oats, plus extra to sprinkle on top
- 125ml Guinness or other Irish stout
- 300ml buttermilk
- 100ml treacle

METHOD

Preheat the oven to 160°C fan/gas 4. Butter and line a 450g loaf tin with baking parchment.

In a large bowl, mix the flours, bicarbonate of soda, salt and oats. Mix the Guinness, buttermilk and treacle in a large jug and pour into the dry ingredients, making sure to scrape the remaining treacle off the jug with a spatula.

Mix well, then scoop the mixture into the prepared loaf tin and top with a sprinkle of oats.

Bake in the oven for 25 minutes, then lower the temperature slightly to 150°C fan/gas 3 and bake for a further 30 minutes.

Make sure the loaf is cooked through by removing from the tin and tapping the bottom – if it sounds hollow it should be cooked. You could always turn it upside down and put it in the oven for a further 5 minutes just to make sure. When finished, take it out of the tin and cool on a wire rack.

The stout and treacle loaf is shown on the left in the picture; the picture also shows kombu butter (see page 173)

Seeded Dillisk Loaf

The combination of seeds, buttermilk and salty dillisk seaweed makes for an unusual bread, both in flavour and appearance. The veins of purple that run through the bread look quite striking, and it's really delicious and earthy. One of our favourite breads to make and eat.

MAKES 8–10 SLICES

- butter, for greasing
- 30g dried dillisk
- 340g wholemeal flour
- 60g sunflower seeds
- 60g pumpkin seeds
- 2 teaspoons bicarbonate of soda
- a pinch of sea salt
- 300ml buttermilk
- 2 medium organic eggs
- 2 tablespoons rapeseed oil

METHOD

Preheat the oven to 210°C fan/gas 8 and butter a 20cm round baking tin.

Finely chop the dillisk. Mix this with the flour, seeds, bicarbonate of soda and salt in a large bowl.

In a large jug, whisk the buttermilk, eggs and rapeseed oil together and pour into the dry ingredients. Using your hand as a claw, stir the mixture in a circular motion until it is well combined.

Pour into the prepared tin and bake in the oven for 40 to 45 minutes. Remove from the tin and pat the bottom – it should sound hollow when it's ready. Cool fully on a wire rack.

The Seeded Dillisk Loaf is shown at the top in the picture on page 39.

Plain Malted Milk Loaf

This is an everyday staple, an easy, versatile bread that's great for toasting and slathering with whatever you fancy. Perfect with soup for a quick lunch or supper. We always keep a loaf or two in the bread bin.

MAKES 2 LOAVES

- 250ml milk
- 25g butter, plus extra for greasing
- 2 tablespoons honey
- 4 tablespoons malt extract
- 300g cream flour, plus extra for dusting
- 150g wholemeal flour
- 1 teaspoon sea salt
- 14g dried yeast

METHOD

In a saucepan, gently heat the milk, butter, honey and malt extract until warm, whisking lightly to incorporate all the ingredients.

In a large bowl, combine both flours, the salt and the yeast. Pour the wet ingredients from the saucepan into the dry ingredients and use your hands to knead it gently in the bowl into a well-combined dough.

Tip on to a lightly floured surface and sprinkle it with flour. Knead gently for 2 to 3 minutes, adding a little more flour if needed.

Butter two 450g loaf tins and divide the dough between them. Cover with a clean tea towel and leave to rise for 2 hours until the dough reaches the top of the tins.

Preheat the oven to 160°C fan/gas 4.

Put the loaves into the oven and bake for 40 to 50 minutes. Keep an eye on them – if they start to brown too much on the top, cover them with tinfoil. Test with a skewer – it should come out clean. Remove from the tins and cool on wire racks.

Thyme and Kombu Focaccia

A classic Italian bread, great for tearing and having with dips or oils. The dried kombu adds a real flavour of the Irish coast, and with the woody aroma of the thyme this is the essence of Currabinny in a bread!

SERVES 4

- 1 tablespoon dried yeast
- 180ml warm water
- 2 tablespoons olive oil, plus extra for greasing and drizzling
- 1 teaspoon honey
- 320g Italian Tipo 00 flour, plus extra for dusting
- 2 teaspoons sea salt, plus extra for the top
- 15g dried kombu, finely chopped
- 5–6 sprigs of fresh thyme

METHOD

In a large jug dissolve the yeast in the warm water and leave for 5 minutes until it starts to get foamy. Add the olive oil and the honey and whisk gently to combine.

Sift the flour into a large mixing bowl and add the 2 teaspoons of salt, the finely chopped kombu and the leaves from the thyme sprigs. Pour the yeast and honey mix into the flour and mix to form a dough.

Tip the dough on to a lightly floured surface and knead for 5 to 10 minutes until smooth, soft and elastic.

Clean the mixing bowl and rub oil all over the inside. Place the dough back in the bowl and cover with a clean cloth. After 30 minutes, tip the dough on to a lightly floured surface again and stretch it into a rectangle shape, folding it and reshaping it three or four times. The dough should now be a very thick small rectangle shape.

Oil a baking sheet (about 25cm x 35cm) and place the folded dough in the middle, cover with a clean tea towel and leave for another hour – it should double in size in this time.

Continued on next page

Once risen, stretch the dough out to cover the baking sheet and sprinkle with extra salt. Cover with a cloth and leave to rest for another 20 minutes before using your fingertips to imprint dents all over the dough.

Drizzle with a little olive oil and leave it to rest for a further 20 minutes. While it's resting, preheat the oven to 180°C fan/gas 6.

Bake in the oven for 25 minutes until golden and crisp-looking. Serve warm, cut into squares.

Macroom Brown Soda Bread

Could there be anything more Irish and down-to-earth than a classic soda bread made with wholewheat flour from the legendary Walton's Mill in Macroom, Co. Cork, Ireland's only surviving stone mill? We don't think so!

MAKES 8–10 SLICES

· butter, for greasing

· 180g cream flour

· 340g Macroom Stoneground Wholewheat Flour (extra coarse)

· 2 teaspoons bicarbonate of soda

· 1 teaspoon sea salt

· 70g Macroom Oatmeal

· 1 medium organic egg

· 575ml buttermilk

METHOD

Preheat the oven to 180°C fan/gas 6. Butter a 450g loaf tin.

In a large mixing bowl, mix the flours, bicarbonate of soda, salt and oatmeal to combine, then make a well in the centre.

Whisk together the egg and buttermilk in a jug, and pour into the dry mix. Using your hand as a claw, mix the ingredients together in a circular motion until well combined.

Pour the mixture into the loaf tin and bake in the oven for 40 to 50 minutes, until a skewer comes out clean. When you remove the loaf from the tin, make sure to tap the bottom too, listening for that hollow sound just to be sure. Cool on a wire rack.

Wholemeal Pitta Bread

Pitta bread is both delicious and incredibly versatile, and it's also surprisingly easy to make at home. The key is to use finely milled wholewheat flour along with the very fine Tipo 00 flour. This combination prevents the dough from becoming too wet and hard to work with.

MAKES 10 PITTAS

- 240ml warm water
- 1 teaspoon honey
- 2 teaspoons dried yeast
- 1 tablespoon olive oil, plus extra for greasing
- 170g wholewheat flour
- 170g Italian Tipo 00 flour, plus extra for dusting
- 1 teaspoon sea salt

METHOD

In a large jug, mix the warm water, honey and yeast and leave for 5 minutes until it starts to get foamy.

Add the olive oil and gently whisk to combine. Mix the two flours with the salt in a large bowl. Pour the yeast and honey mixture into the flour and bring together with your hands to form a dough.

Turn out your dough on to a lightly floured surface and knead for 5 to 10 minutes until the dough is smooth.

Clean out your mixing bowl and rub oil lightly all over the inside. Form the dough into a ball and put it into the bowl, then cover with a clean tea towel and leave to rise for about an hour.

Knock back the dough and divide into 10 individual balls. Roll out each ball on a lightly floured surface until you have 5mm-thick rounds. Leave on a floured surface and cover with a damp cloth for 20 minutes while you preheat the oven to 210°C fan/gas 8.

Cook 3 or 4 at a time in the oven on an oiled baking sheet for around 5 minutes (or you could put in two baking sheets at the same time), until the pitta breads start to balloon and turn light golden in colour. Cool and serve.

Irish Cider and Honey Loaf

The combination of yeast, really dry cider and honey gives this bread a distinctive tartness with an undercurrent of mellow sweetness. Lovely at any time of the year, but particularly comforting when the leaves start changing colour and the days are getting shorter.

MAKES 12–15 SLICES

- 150ml milk
- 2 teaspoons honey
- 30g fresh yeast
- 250g strong white flour, plus extra for dusting
- 250g Macroom Stoneground Wholewheat Flour (extra coarse)
- 1 teaspoon sea salt
- 250ml dry Irish cider, such as Longueville or Llewellyn's
- olive or rapeseed oil, for greasing

METHOD

Gently warm the milk and honey in a small saucepan – you should be able to place a finger in the milk and comfortably leave it there without burning yourself. Take off the heat and crumble the yeast in, stirring with a fork. Leave for 5 to 7 minutes until the milk is biscuit-coloured and foamy.

In a large bowl, mix the two flours and the salt. Pour the milk mixture into the flour mixture and then pour the cider in, using a wooden spoon to mix the ingredients as you go. A sticky dough should form.

Tip on to a lightly floured surface and knead for at least 5 minutes or until the dough is relatively smooth. You will need to sprinkle more flour on to the dough, but try not to add too much. The dough will be sticky and hard to handle, but stick with it!

Clean out your mixing bowl and rub oil lightly all over the inside. Place the dough in the bowl, cover with a clean tea towel and leave to rise in a warm place for around 1 hour. After this time the dough should have doubled in size.

Tip on to a lightly floured surface once again and knead for 1 to 2 minutes. Return the dough to the bowl and leave covered for a further 30 minutes until it has risen again.

Preheat the oven to 180°C fan/gas 6. Line a baking sheet with baking parchment and <u>lightly</u> flour it.

Flip the dough once more on to a lightly floured surface and knock back, then knead lightly and form into a smooth ball. Place on the baking sheet, lightly flour the top and cover with the tea towel to rise for another 20 minutes while the oven
heats up.

Bake in the oven for 25 to 30 minutes until brown and the crust is starting to tear and split at the top. Using a tea towel, flip the bread over and tap the bottom – if there's a good hollow sound then your bread is done.

Cool on a wire rack before slicing.

Rosemary, Apple and Buttermilk Loaf

Rosemary is both pungent and woody, giving this loaf a lovely earthy flavour. It's an intriguing combination of savoury and sweet, so it's perfect for guests who don't have a very sweet tooth. It combines lovely sharp apples and the tang of buttermilk along with the rosemary. Go gently with the rosemary the first time you bake this and then you can adjust the level to suit to your taste.

MAKES 8–10 SLICES

· butter, for greasing

· 65g wholemeal spelt flour

· 65g cream flour

· 2 teaspoons baking powder

· a pinch of sea salt

· 80g golden caster sugar, plus extra to sprinkle on top

· 2 teaspoons finely chopped fresh rosemary, or to taste

· zest of 1 lemon

· 150ml buttermilk

· 60ml rapeseed oil

· 1 medium organic egg

· 1 large cooking apple

METHOD

Preheat the oven to 160°C fan/gas 4. Butter a 450g loaf tin.

In a large bowl, mix the flours, baking powder, salt, sugar, rosemary and lemon zest. Whisk the buttermilk, rapeseed oil and egg in a large jug. Peel and core the apple, and chop into small pieces.

Make a well in the centre of the flour mixture and pour in the wet ingredients from the jug. Mix gently until smooth, then fold in the apple pieces.

Pour the mixture into the loaf tin, sprinkle a little golden caster sugar on top and place in the oven for around 40 minutes. When a skewer comes out clean, the loaf should be done – you want a nice pale golden colour on top.

Leave to cool in the tin for 10 minutes before gently flipping the loaf out to cool further on a wire rack. You can serve it warm if you like, with a little butter.

The rosemary, apple and buttermilk loaf is shown to the right in the picture on page 39

SOUP

Parsnip and Fennel Soup

In this soup the natural sweetness of parsnip combines beautifully with the delicate aniseed flavour of fennel. The result is smooth, velvety and very elegant.

SERVES 4–6

- 1 medium-sized onion
- 4 medium-sized parsnips
- 2 large fennel bulbs, stalks removed
- 1 stick of celery
- 15g fresh flat-leaf parsley
- 70g butter
- sea salt and freshly ground black pepper
- 1½ litres vegetable stock
- 200ml milk

TO SERVE:

- fresh cream
- fresh fennel fronds

METHOD

Peel the onion and parsnips. Chop finely, together with the fennel bulbs and celery, to roughly the same size dice. Roughly chop the parsley leaves.

Melt the butter in a large pot or casserole dish. Add the onion, parsnips, fennel and celery, and season well with salt and pepper. Stir so that everything in the pot is well coated in the butter.

Construct a cartouche by cutting a circle of greaseproof paper which perfectly covers the inside of your pot. Press this down on the vegetables, sealing them in to cook. Put the lid on the pot and cook for around 10 minutes on a gentle heat. Check and stir at least once to make sure nothing is catching on the bottom.

Meanwhile, in another pot, heat up your vegetable stock until it comes to the boil. This will shorten the cooking time considerably.

When it's boiling, remove the cartouche from the other pot and pour your hot stock over the vegetables, stirring the contents to make sure nothing is stuck to the bottom.

Simmer on a medium heat for around 20 minutes until the vegetables are completely soft and tender.

Add the milk and parsley, and blend with a stick blender until completely smooth and creamy.

Check the seasoning and serve with a swirl of cream and some fennel fronds sprinkled on top of each bowl.

Very Green Asparagus Soup

Though we share a love of food and experimentation, William is the chef in the house and James is more the sous-chef. However, James has his star recipes too, and this asparagus soup is a favourite – just the ticket when you are craving a big bowl of green goodness.

SERVES 2–3

- 350g asparagus
- 3 shallots
- 2 cloves of garlic
- 25g butter
- a dash of rapeseed oil
- 2 large handfuls of spinach
- 700ml vegetable stock
- sea salt and freshly ground black pepper

TO SERVE:

- crème fraîche
- olive oil

METHOD

Remove the woody ends from the asparagus spears, then chop the stalks into 2cm pieces and reserve the tips. Peel and finely slice the shallots, and peel and crush the garlic.

Put the butter and rapeseed oil into a large saucepan on a medium-high heat. When foaming, add the asparagus tips and fry for a few minutes to soften. Remove the asparagus tips and set aside.

Add the shallots, asparagus stalks and garlic to the pan, and cook for 5 to 10 minutes until softened but still bright in colour.

Next, stir through the spinach, pour over the stock and bring to the boil. Remove from the heat and blitz with a hand blender. Season generously with salt and pepper, and add some hot water to loosen if needed.

Ladle into bowls and swirl through some crème fraîche or drizzle some olive oil. Scatter the asparagus tips over each serving and serve with chunks of bread.

Vegetable Broth with Chard and Orzo

This is a gorgeous, hearty, healthy soup, featuring one of William's favourite vegetables, chard, and also orzo – a tiny pasta shape that looks like rice – to give it extra body. It's totally comforting and fills the belly nicely on a chilly night!

SERVES 2

- 2 leeks
- 3 cloves of garlic
- 3 medium-sized carrots
- 2 sticks of celery
- 4 medium-sized potatoes
- 30g butter
- olive oil
- sea salt and freshly ground black pepper
- 500ml vegetable stock, or more if you prefer
- 2 bay leaves
- 4 sprigs of fresh thyme
- 100g orzo pasta
- 3 tablespoons chopped fresh flat-leaf parsley
- 250g chard, stalks removed, leaves washed
- juice of ½ a lemon

METHOD

Remove the green part of the leeks (keep aside for stocks and soups), then wash the white part and chop into 2cm rounds. Peel and slice the garlic. Cut the carrots and celery into large chunks, keeping them separate, and peel and cut the potatoes into medium-sized chunks.

Put the butter and a little drizzle of olive oil into a heavy-bottomed saucepan or casserole dish on a medium heat. Add the leeks, garlic and celery and season well with salt and pepper.

After 5 minutes, add the potatoes and carrots and cook for another 5 minutes, stirring everything occasionally. Allow the vegetables to brown slightly and stick to the bottom every now and then.

Bring the stock to the boil in a separate pot, then pour this over the browned vegetables. Add the bay leaves and thyme, and simmer for about 20 minutes until everything is tender. If you feel you'd like more liquid in your broth, you can always add a little more stock to taste.

Add the orzo, 2 tablespoons of the chopped parsley and the chard leaves (tear the larger ones), and cook for another 10 minutes or until the orzo is al dente. Add the lemon juice and the rest of the parsley.

Check the seasoning, and serve hot with some hunks of good buttered bread.

Chicken Broth with Potato, Spring Onion and Courgette

Everyone knows that chicken broth is the ultimate cure-all. This version has a lighter, more spring–summer feel than other recipes – but it's just as comforting and restorative.

SERVES 2–4

FOR THE CHICKEN STOCK:

- 1 free-range chicken carcass, leftover meat removed
- 1 stick of celery, chopped
- 1 carrot, chopped into thick rounds
- 1 large onion, peeled and quartered
- 3–4 black peppercorns
- 1 bay leaf
- 1 sprig of fresh thyme
- sea salt and freshly ground black pepper

FOR THE FINISHED BROTH:

- 2 medium-sized floury potatoes, such as Red Rooster
- 2 courgettes
- 6 spring onions
- 1 tablespoon olive oil
- 25g butter
- as much leftover chicken as you have
- fresh chives, to garnish

METHOD

First prepare the stock. Place the chicken carcass in a large, heavy-based saucepan and cover with 1½ to 2 litres of cold water. Bring to the boil and add the rest of the stock ingredients. Bring to the boil again, then reduce to a rolling simmer and leave to bubble away with a lid askew for about an hour. You can add more water if necessary.

Now reduce the heat to low and leave to simmer gently for another 40 minutes to an hour. Strain the broth into a bowl, so you are left with a delicious concentrated stock. You'll get about 1 to 1½ litres.

If you're not eating straight away, you can leave it to cool, put it in the fridge and skim off any excess fat that rises to the top when you get the chance – though we don't mind a little fat personally!

To make the finished broth, peel the potatoes and chop into chunks, then chop the courgettes into similar-sized chunks and thinly slice the spring onions.

Put the olive oil and the butter into a heavy casserole dish over a medium heat. Add the potatoes and courgettes, and soften for around 5 minutes.

Throw in the leftover chicken, add 500ml of your chicken stock and bring to the boil. Reduce the heat to a simmer and leave for 10 to 15 minutes until the potatoes are cooked. When the potatoes are nearly ready, add the spring onions and cook for a minute or two.

Divide between your bowls, garnishing with some roughly chopped chives.

Coconut and Lime Soup
with Hake and Coriander

Hake tastes so delicate that it can easily be overpowered if it's put
with strong flavours. The South East Asian ingredients in this soup –
coconut milk, lime, coriander, fish sauce – make it light and tangy
and are the perfect accompaniment to the fresh clean flavour of the
fish. It's a beautiful aromatic soup that you'll return to again and again.

SERVES 2–3

- 1 x 400ml tin of organic
  coconut milk
- 150ml vegetable stock
- 1 tablespoon fish sauce
- juice of 1 lime
- 2 x 150g hake fillets,
  cut into chunks
- sea salt and freshly
  ground black pepper
- a handful of fresh
  coriander leaves
- 2 spring onions

METHOD

In a large saucepan, heat the coconut milk, vegetable
stock, fish sauce and lime juice until they come to
the boil. Season the hake chunks with salt and pepper
and add to the pan, reducing the heat to a simmer.

Cook for 5 to 10 minutes.

Roughly chop the coriander, finely slice the spring
onions and sprinkle them over the soup. Serve piping
hot in large bowls, with chunks of rustic bread.

Cleansing Nettle Broth

As this is light and delicate, it's best to use only young nettle leaves and buds, which will give a gentle texture and flavour.

SERVES 4–6

- 4 onions
- 3 leeks
- 1 stalk of celery
- 100g young spring nettle leaves
- a small bunch of fresh chives
- 3 tablespoons olive oil
- 1½ litres water
- sea salt and freshly ground black pepper

METHOD

Peel and slice the onions. Remove the green part of the leeks (keep aside for stocks and soups), then wash the white part and slice into 1–2cm pieces.

Slice the celery into 1–2cm pieces. Wash the nettle leaves and chop the chives.

Pour the olive oil into a large saucepan and place on a medium heat. Add the onions, leeks and celery, and sauté gently until softened. Add the water, season with salt and pepper, bring to the boil and simmer for around 35 minutes.

Add the nettle leaves and chives (reserving some of the chives for later) and cook for a further 5 minutes. Serve hot, sprinkled generously with the remaining chives.

SALAD

Baked Feta, Roasted Lemon and Trofie Salad with Sesame Toasts

Imagine a large bowl filled with the freshest, brightest and most colourful ingredients, each one offering a different taste and texture – that's this salad, bursting with the flavour of summertime.

SERVES 4 AS A LIGHT LUNCH, 2 AS A MAIN MEAL

- 300g trofie pasta
- 2 lemons, sliced into thin rounds
- olive oil
- sea salt
- 2 sprigs of fresh marjoram
- 1 small raw beetroot
- juice of 1 lemon
- 2 tablespoons white wine vinegar
- 1 tablespoon honey
- 150g radishes, quartered
- 1 small red onion, sliced thinly
- 50g rocket
- a handful of fresh basil leaves
- a handful of fresh flat-leaf parsley leaves
- a handful of fresh dill, chopped
- a few cornflowers, to garnish (optional)

METHOD

Preheat the oven to 200°C fan/gas 7.

Cook the trofie pasta in salted boiling water until al dente. Drain and rinse with cold water to stop the pasta from cooking further. Set aside.

Lay out the lemon slices on a roasting tray, drizzle with olive oil, season with salt and place the sprigs of marjoram on top. Put into the oven for 20 minutes or until caramelized. Keep an eye on them so they don't burn!

While the lemon slices are in the oven, scrub, top and tail and slice the beetroot as thinly as possible. Lay the slices on a plate, mix together the lemon juice, white wine vinegar and honey with a little salt, and drizzle over. Leave to marinate for 30 minutes. When the lemon slices are ready, remove them from the oven and leave to cool, but don't turn the oven off yet.

Make the dressing by whisking all the ingredients together with a pinch or two of salt. In a large bowl, mix together the cooked trofie, radishes, onion, rocket, most of the basil, parsley and dill, and the cooled lemon slices. Stir the dressing through gently, along with the beetroot slices.

Continued on page 72

FOR THE DRESSING:

· zest of 1 orange

· 100ml olive oil

· 4 tablespoons lemon juice

FOR THE BAKED FETA:

· 200g feta cheese

· a few fresh
  marjoram leaves

FOR THE SESAME TOASTS:

· 2 cloves of garlic

· a small handful of fresh
  flat-leaf parsley leaves

· 50g butter, softened

· juice of ½ a small lemon

· 2 tablespoons sesame seeds

· 4 slices of sourdough bread

Cut the feta into large chunks and place in an ovenproof dish. Drizzle with olive oil and sprinkle with the marjoram leaves. Bake for about 10 minutes, until soft.

While the feta is cooking, make the sesame toasts. Peel and crush the garlic, chop the parsley and mash these into the butter with some salt and the lemon juice. Melt in a shallow pan and add the sesame seeds.

When the seeds turn golden, turn the heat to moderate and add the bread to the pan, coating it in the sesame seeds. Cook both sides until crisp and golden. Drain on paper towels.

Assemble the salad on a large plate. Arrange the warm baked feta in the middle, garnish with cornflowers and the leftover herb leaves, and serve with the sesame toasts.

Crushed New Potatoes with Pink Peppercorns, Capers and Parsley

New potatoes have thinner skins, a waxier texture and a sweeter flavour than older types and are therefore perfectly suited to salads. This recipe keeps things simple and shows them off to best effect.

SERVES 6 AS A
GENEROUS SIDE

- 1kg new potatoes, unpeeled
- 2 cloves of garlic
- 4 spring onions, white parts only
- 300g Greek yoghurt
- 100ml olive oil
- 30g fresh flat-leaf parsley, leaves picked and chopped
- 1 tablespoon chopped fresh chives
- 1 tablespoon pink peppercorns
- 2 tablespoons capers
- sea salt and freshly ground black pepper

METHOD

Wash the new potatoes in cold water and put them into a pan. Cover with water and add plenty of salt. Bring to the boil and simmer for 20 to 25 minutes until a knife can go through them with just a little resistance.

Drain the cooked potatoes, place in a large mixing bowl and crush roughly with a fork.

Peel and crush the garlic, then slice the spring onions. Mix the yoghurt, olive oil and crushed garlic together in a small bowl. Add this mixture to the potatoes and stir, making sure to coat all the potatoes.

Stir in the parsley, chives, spring onions, pink peppercorns and capers, and season with salt and pepper before serving.

Smoked Mackerel with Tabasco and Lime Potato Salad

Robust flavours and textures make this salad punchy and distinctive. Use as much or as little Tabasco as you can handle!

SERVES 4

- 340g new potatoes
- zest and juice of 1 lime
- a pinch of pink peppercorns

FOR THE DRESSING:

- a handful of fresh flat-leaf parsley leaves
- a handful of fresh coriander leaves
- juice of 1 lemon
- 3 anchovies
- 1 teaspoon Dijon mustard
- a few drops of Tabasco
- 1 clove of garlic, peeled
- 1 tablespoon white wine vinegar
- sea salt and freshly ground black pepper
- 2 tablespoons olive oil

TO SERVE:

- 2 smoked mackerel fillets
- 1 lime
- a handful of fresh coriander leaves, chopped

METHOD

Cut the potatoes in half, place in a large saucepan and cover with cold salted water. Bring to the boil and simmer for 15 minutes or until cooked through.

Drain and toss with the lime juice and zest.

Blitz all the dressing ingredients in a food processor, adding more olive oil if needed to get a good pouring consistency. Put the potatoes into a large bowl, drizzle generously with the dressing and sprinkle over the pink peppercorns.

Pull the smoked mackerel fillets gently apart into large pieces and arrange on top with wedges of lime and some chopped coriander.

Balsamic Cucumber with Kalamata Olives

Bright, salty, complex flavours make this salad an addictive and healthy lunch. It's great on its own, but also delicious with focaccia or other good bread and some beetroot and seaweed hummus (see page 164). It also works very well with barbecued mackerel (see page 144). To get so much taste packed into something that's so simple to create makes it extra rewarding!

SERVES 4–6

- 2 cucumbers
- 2 spring onions
- 2 tablespoons balsamic vinegar
- 1 tablespoon olive oil
- sea salt and freshly ground black pepper
- juice of ½ a lemon
- 8–10 Kalamata olives, unstoned*
- 1 tablespoon chopped fresh dill

METHOD

Cut the cucumbers in half lengthways and use a teaspoon to gouge out the watery seeds. Chop the cucumber halves into good-sized chunks. Finely slice the spring onions.

In a medium-sized bowl, whisk together the balsamic vinegar, olive oil, some salt and pepper and the lemon juice until well combined. Put the cucumber chunks into this bowl with the olives, sliced spring onions and dill. Cover with cling film and leave to marinate in the fridge for at least 30 minutes before serving.

Unless making something like a tapenade, we leave olives unstoned to preserve all the flavours and juices until the moment of eating.

Yellow and Green Courgetti with Toasted Almonds and Feta

In Currabinny we always grew too many courgettes, so we have a lot of courgette recipes! In this salad you are effectively 'cooking' the flesh in the acid of the lemon juice. It's a perfect way to enjoy courgette, as it retains its bright summery flavour and crunchy texture.

SERVES 4

· 2 green courgettes
· 1 yellow courgette
· sea salt and freshly ground black pepper
· 1 tablespoon rapeseed oil
· juice of 1 lemon
· a handful of fresh mint leaves
· a handful of fresh basil leaves
· 1 tablespoon pink peppercorns
· 200g feta cheese
· 50g flaked almonds

METHOD

Trim the courgettes and spiralize into flat, long ribbons. If you don't own a spiralizer, you can use a vegetable peeler instead.

In a large bowl, mix the courgette ribbons with a good pinch of salt, some pepper, the rapeseed oil and the lemon juice. Leave for 10 minutes to let the lemon juice 'cook' the courgettes.

Chop the mint and basil leaves and add these to the courgettes, along with the pink peppercorns. Crumble in the feta.

Put a frying pan on a medium-high heat and add the flaked almonds. Keep the almonds moving in the pan for around 2 minutes, until they start to turn golden around the edges and you can smell them. Remove from the pan and add to the salad bowl. This salad is best served while the almonds are still warm.

The yellow and green courgetti salad is shown on page 68

Chicory Salad with Pomegranate, Grilled Halloumi and Lime Dressing

The bitterness of chicory can make it difficult to work with. Using a zingy dressing – like this lime and balsamic mix – balances the bitterness beautifully. The halloumi turns this salad into a proper meal – its saltiness can hold its own in this symphony of intense flavours!

SERVES 4 AS A SIDE DISH OR 2 AS A MAIN

- 3 small radishes
- 2 heads of white chicory
- 1 head of red chicory
- 100g rocket
- 50g walnuts, chopped roughly
- 1 pomegranate

FOR THE DRESSING:
- juice of 1 lime
- 2 tablespoons rapeseed oil
- a pinch of sea salt and freshly ground black pepper
- 1 tablespoon chopped fresh coriander leaves
- 1 tablespoon balsamic vinegar

FOR THE HALLOUMI:
- 225g halloumi cheese
- rapeseed oil
- 1 lime

METHOD

Trim and thinly slice the radishes. Cut the ends off the heads of chicory, cut in half lengthways and separate the leaves. Put the radishes and chicory into a large salad bowl with the rocket and chopped walnuts.

Slice the pomegranate in half and hold one of the halves, cut side down, over the bowl. With your hand covering the cut half, beat the back of the pomegranate with a wooden spoon so the seeds fall in between your fingers into the bowl. Make sure to remove any bits of white pith that fall into the salad. Repeat with the other half.

Whisk together the dressing ingredients until well combined and pour into a jar or dressing bottle.

Slice the halloumi into chunky 2cm-sized pieces. Heat a little rapeseed oil in a frying pan or griddle until the pan is very hot, then turn the heat down to medium. Fry the halloumi in batches for around 2 minutes on each side, being careful not to let it burn. Squeeze lime juice over both sides of the halloumi pieces as you cook them.

Arrange the salad on plates, top with the hot halloumi and drizzle with the dressing.

Orzo with Preserved Lemon and Thyme Cream

This is a really elegant pasta dish that can be served hot, or cold as a salad. The sumac is colourful, slightly bitter and wonderfully fragrant, and it, along with the salty preserved lemon, gives this dish an exotic edge.

SERVES 4

- 350g orzo pasta

FOR THE PRESERVED LEMON AND THYME CREAM:

- 1 shallot
- skin of ½ a preserved lemon
- olive oil
- 250ml double cream or crème fraîche
- sea salt and freshly ground black pepper
- 1 tablespoon fresh thyme leaves
- 1 teaspoon sumac

METHOD

To make the cream, peel and finely chop the shallot, then finely chop the lemon skin. Put a little olive oil into a frying pan, add the shallot and cook for 2 minutes on a medium heat to soften. Add the preserved lemon and stir for another 2 minutes until fragrant.

Pour in the double cream and leave to cook for 5 minutes until bubbling, then season the cream with salt and pepper and add the thyme leaves. Cook for a further 5 minutes, at which point the cream will start to thicken.

Take off the heat and stir in the sumac.

Cook the orzo as per the packet instructions, then drain, and pour the sauce over, mixing thoroughly.

Citrus Salad with Honeyed Buttermilk

When William was growing up there was always some buttermilk in the fridge, so it's very much part of the Currabinny story. Finding uses for it apart from in baking can be hard, but here it goes wonderfully with fruit. Think of this as a breakfast salad – combining juicy citrus fruit with the sweet but tangy buttermilk.

SERVES 2

- 1 pink grapefruit
- 1 yellow grapefruit
- 2 blood oranges
- 2 large Seville oranges
- a few chopped fresh mint or basil leaves, to serve

FOR THE HONEYED BUTTERMILK DRESSING:

- 120ml buttermilk
- ½ teaspoon vanilla extract
- 2 tablespoons honey
- 3 tablespoons natural yoghurt
- juice of ½ a lemon
- 1 tablespoon peanut oil
- a pinch of sea salt

METHOD

Using a sharp knife, slice the tops and bottoms off each of the citrus fruits, then stand them up on your chopping board. Slice or peel away their peel and pith until just the flesh remains.

Turn each fruit on its side and slice into ½cm rounds. Arrange in a single layer on a large platter or two plates.

Whisk all the ingredients for the honeyed buttermilk dressing together in a bowl and pour into a serving jug. Pour a little of the dressing over the fruit and sprinkle with the chopped mint or basil leaves.

Hedgerow Berry Salad
with Lime Syrup

Blackberry-picking is part of every Irish country childhood –
hedgerows heavy with fruit, purple-stained fingers, faces and clothes,
the odd prick of a thumb! Combined with the other fruit and drizzled
with a tangy syrup made from a sweet herb, this is about as simple
as it gets, a real celebration of berries. As it's so fresh and easy, we've
included this in our salad section, but you'll probably serve it as a
refreshing dessert. Still, there's nothing to stop you having it for
breakfast or lunch!

SERVES 4

- 300g fresh hedgerow
  blackberries
- 100g redcurrants
- 50g strawberries
- 50g raspberries
- 5–6 fresh mint leaves

FOR THE SYRUP:

- 150ml water
- 150g caster sugar
- 4–5 sweet geranium
  leaves (mint, lemon
  balm or sweet cicely
  leaves also work well)
- juice and peel of 1 lime

METHOD

Wash all the berries, then remove the stems from the
strawberries and cut them into quarters. Assemble the
berries on a large platter or in a bowl. Chop the mint
finely and sprinkle over the berries.

Make the syrup by heating the water and sugar up
to boiling point. Turn the heat down, add the geranium
leaves and lime peel and simmer for 5 minutes. Take
off the heat and add the lime juice, stirring it through
to combine. Leave to cool.

Serve the berries with a jug of the syrup on the side, so that
people can pour it over the fruit themselves.

Fresh Figs with Black Pepper and Honey

How beautiful and perfect are figs? When ripe they are sticky, sweet and heavy with flavour. Here they're sliced thinly – skin and all – and dressed with warm peppery honey to create the perfect amuse-bouche or starter for a summer dinner.

SERVES 4–6

- 8–10 fresh figs
- 100ml honey
- 4–5 sprigs of fresh thyme
- 1 teaspoon freshly ground black pepper

METHOD

Twist the stems off the figs and cut each one into 3 or 4 slices. Or you can cut a cross from the top down to the base, without cutting through, and open out into quarters. Arrange on a platter.

In a small saucepan, gently heat the honey, sprigs of thyme and black pepper until just about simmering.

Drizzle directly over the fig slices and serve.

VEGETABLE
& PASTA MAINS

Cavolo Nero, Feta and Butternut Squash Filo Pie

This is a hearty, comforting pie that makes the most of winter vegetables and has a gentle kick of chilli heat. It's particularly great for dinner when the days are closing in and it's cold and wet.

MAKES 8 GOOD-SIZED SLICES

- 1 large butternut squash (about 900g unpeeled weight)
- 2 medium-sized red onions
- 4 cloves of garlic
- 1 small fresh red chilli
- olive oil
- sea salt and freshly ground black pepper
- 15g fresh rosemary spears
- 400g cavolo nero
- 200g feta cheese
- 4 sheets of filo pastry
- melted butter, for brushing the pastry

METHOD

Preheat the oven to 200°C fan/gas 7.

Peel the squash, scoop out any seeds and cut the flesh into bite-sized pieces – you should get around 500g of flesh. Peel and slice the onions and garlic. Finely chop the chilli, removing the seeds if you don't like too much heat.

Place the butternut squash, red onions and chilli in an even layer on a baking tray, drizzle with olive oil and season with salt and pepper. Pick and chop the rosemary leaves, scatter them over the top and bake in the oven for 20 minutes until the butternut squash is tender. Leave the oven on for baking the pie.

While the squash is roasting, wash and roughly chop the cavolo nero, removing the heavy stalks. Cook with a good splash of water and a sprinkle of salt in a heavy-based saucepan until thoroughly wilted but still dark green. Squeeze out the moisture using kitchen paper.

Place the roasted veg in the bottom of a casserole dish, scatter with the cavolo nero and crumble the feta on top.

Cover with the filo pastry, cutting away any excess pieces you don't need. Brush the top with a little melted butter and place in the oven for 15 minutes until the pastry is golden. Serve immediately.

Rustic Rye Galette with Leeks, Fennel, Goat's Cheese and Toasted Pine Nuts

You construct this traditional free-form savoury tart by rolling out the pastry into a large round, dolloping the buttery filling in the middle, and gathering up the pastry around the filling to form a border, not caring if things are uneven or if a piece breaks off. This is a celebration of simple, unfussy, hands-on cooking at its best.

SERVES 4–6

FOR THE RYE PASTRY:
- 80g cream flour
- 90g rye flour
- 1 teaspoon caster sugar
- ½ teaspoon sea salt
- 1 medium organic egg
- 40ml double cream
- 120g cold butter
- 2 teaspoons lemon juice
- ½ teaspoon lemon zest

FOR THE FILLING:
- 4 medium-sized leeks
- 2 fennel bulbs
- 15g butter
- olive oil
- 2 teaspoons fresh thyme leaves, plus extra for sprinkling
- sea salt and freshly ground black pepper
- 60ml white wine
- 60ml double cream
- 2 tablespoons chopped fresh flat-leaf parsley leaves
- 150g soft goat's cheese, such as St Tola or Ardsallagh
- toasted pine nuts, to garnish

METHOD

First, make the pastry dough. Combine the two flours, sugar and salt in a large mixing bowl. Whisk the egg with the cream in a large jug. Cut the butter into small chunks and rub into the flour mix until you have a breadcrumb-like consistency.

Drizzle the egg and cream mixture into the crumbs slowly, mixing it with your hands as you go. You may not need all the egg and cream – you are looking for a smooth dough that comes together nicely without sticking to everything.

Reserve a small amount of the cream mixture for finishing the galette later. Add the lemon juice and zest to the dough and knead in, sprinkling more flour on if it becomes too wet. Shape the dough into a disc, cover with cling film and refrigerate for at least 2 hours.

Preheat the oven to 200°C fan/gas 7.

Remove the green part of the leeks (keep aside for stocks and soups), then wash the white part and slice into 1cm rounds. Finely slice the fennel. In a heavy-bottomed saucepan, heat the butter with a little olive oil and add the leeks, fennel and thyme leaves. Season with salt and pepper and cook on a medium heat for around 10 minutes until everything is nicely softened.

Add the white wine and continue cooking until it has reduced, then add the cream and parsley. Cook until the sauce is nicely coating the leeks and fennel and isn't too runny. Take off the heat and leave to cool.

Roll the pastry out into a big round about ½cm thick on a large baking tray (about 40cm x 35cm) lined with baking parchment. Cut off any excess dough – the pastry should be roughly 30cm in diameter.

Spread the leek and fennel mixture in the middle of the dough, leaving a good 5cm gap along the edges. Spoon dollops of goat's cheese all over the top, then sprinkle with salt and pepper and some more thyme leaves.

Fold the uncovered dough in on itself until you have a rustic, rough-and-ready open pie. Use the remaining egg and cream to brush the dough, then place in the oven for around 40 minutes until golden and bubbling. Sprinkle the toasted pine nuts over before serving.

Homemade Gnocchi with Buffalo Mozzarella, Pickled Walnuts and Green Herb and Lemon Dressing

Sometimes you come across pickled walnuts on a dusty shelf, as a kind of oddity. However, there's nothing odd about the flavour – it is a wonderful combination of sweet and tangy nuttiness. In this recipe it pairs beautifully with mozzarella and a herby dressing. Making gnocchi is so simple, it is a shame anyone buys them pre-made.

SERVES 4

- 500g floury potatoes, such as Maris Piper
- 125g Italian Tipo 00 flour, plus extra for dusting
- 4 buffalo mozzarella balls
- 2 pickled walnuts, sliced
- 2 tablespoons grated pecorino
- green herb and lemon dressing (see page 177 – use the full quantity from that recipe)

METHOD

Peel the potatoes and boil them in salted water for around 30 minutes until cooked through. Drain, then use a wooden spoon to push the potatoes through a fine-mesh sieve into a bowl.

Gently sprinkle the flour in batches into the mashed potato, folding through to combine each time until you are left with an elastic, dough-like mash.

Lightly flour a board and roll the dough out into long sausages, roughly the circumference of a butcher's sausage. Cut the sausages into 3cm pieces and place on a floured plate or tray until ready to use. Cover with cling film so they don't dry out.

Bring a large, heavy-bottomed saucepan of salted water to the boil and cook the gnocchi in batches, 10 or 12 at a time, so you don't overcrowd the pan.

The gnocchi cook quickly – you will know they are ready when they float and bob on the surface of the water. Drain on paper towels when done.

Divide the gnocchi into bowls, then tear over the mozzarella into large pieces. Sprinkle with the sliced pickled walnuts and grated pecorino, and drizzle generously with the green herb and lemon dressing.

Baked Potatoes with Ricotta and Green Herb and Lemon Dressing

This recipe takes the lonely image of the baked potato dinner and makes it the treat it truly is. Between creamy ricotta and a lovely sharp dressing packed with herby freshness, in this version the floury flesh of the potato gets the kind of celebratory treatment it deserves.

SERVES 4

- 4 good-sized floury potatoes, such as Rooster or Kerr's Pink
- olive oil
- sea salt and freshly ground pepper
- 1 clove of garlic
- 5–6 fresh chives
- 250g buffalo ricotta
- green herb and lemon dressing (see page 177 – use the full quantity from that recipe)

METHOD

Preheat the oven to 200°C fan/gas 7.

Prick the potatoes several times with a fork and rub all over with olive oil. Place on a baking tray, sprinkle with salt and bake in the oven for 1 hour.

When the potatoes are done, remove from the oven, cut in half and scoop out a little of the flesh of each potato half. Return the potato halves to the oven for another 8 minutes.

Peel and finely chop the garlic, chop the chives and combine in a bowl with the scooped-out potato and ricotta. Season with salt and pepper.

Remove the potato halves from the oven and fill each half with the ricotta mix, then return to the oven for a final 10 minutes. Serve hot with the dressing spooned over.

Ruby Chard Korma

William's mother, Breda, has always kept a patch of ground at Currabinny for the largely unsuccessful cultivation of vegetables, berries and fruit trees. The combination of salty gale-force winds from Cork Harbour and the relentless encroachment of tree roots from Currabinny Woods just behind the house present her with some serious challenges. However, among the fruitless plum trees, the gooseberry bushes with their bitter, unripe berries, and the small, flattened carrot tops, one thing grows in abundance: chard. Thus, in Currabinny, chard gets put into every dish imaginable.

Chard is a highly nutritious leaf, commonly used in the same way as spinach, although it's more closely related to beetroot. William didn't see chard much after moving to Dublin (though it's more common now), so, in a fit of nostalgic enthusiasm when he came across it, and with an unshakable belief that chard works in anything, he decided to add it to a korma. And the result was amazing – as he knew it would be!

Continued on next page

SERVES 4–6

- 3 onions
- 3 cloves of garlic
- a thumb-sized piece of fresh ginger
- 700g chestnut mushrooms
- a large knob of butter
- sea salt and freshly ground black pepper
- seeds from 10 cardamom pods, crushed
- 1 teaspoon ground cumin
- 1 teaspoon ground turmeric
- a few pinches of ground cinnamon
- a few pinches of chilli powder
- 3 bay leaves
- 200ml water
- 350g ruby chard
- 200g natural yoghurt
- 150g crème fraîche

TO SERVE:

- toasted flaked almonds
- pomegranate seeds
- basmati rice

METHOD

Peel the onions, garlic and ginger. Slice the onions and mushrooms, grate the ginger and crush the garlic with some salt. Melt the butter in a large pan and add the onions, garlic and ginger with some salt and pepper.

When the onions have softened a bit, add the cardamom, cumin, turmeric, cinnamon, chilli powder and bay leaves. Now add the sliced mushrooms to the pan and cook for a couple of minutes, stirring regularly. Pour in the water, stir, and simmer for 15 minutes, then check the seasoning.

Meanwhile, remove the stalks from the chard* and add the leaves in batches to the pot until it is all wilted. Turn the heat to low and gently stir in the yoghurt and crème fraîche.

Serve with rice and top with the almonds and pomegranate seeds.

Don't throw away the stalks! You can use them to make stock (they'll keep in the freezer), but they are also really nice chopped roughly, sautéed with butter and served as a side dish with a main course.

Chard and Ricotta Lasagne

This is a break from the traditional lasagne, which has a lot of elements and involves a lot of cooking. Of course, a classic lasagne is lovely, but this veggie version is quick, easy and just as tasty.

SERVES 6–8

- 400g rainbow chard
- 400g chestnut mushrooms
- 3 cloves of garlic
- sea salt and freshly ground black pepper
- 50g butter
- 1 tablespoon fresh thyme leaves
- a small handful of fresh flat-leaf parsley leaves, chopped
- 200g hard goat's cheese, such as aged Ardsallagh
- 2 medium organic eggs
- 300g buffalo ricotta
- 300ml single cream
- ¼ teaspoon freshly grated nutmeg
- zest of ½ a small lemon
- 180g dried lasagne sheets

METHOD

Preheat the oven to 180°C fan/gas 6.

Wash the chard, remove the heavy stalks and shred the leaves. Wipe and thinly slice the mushrooms, then peel and slice the cloves of garlic.

Place the chard leaves in a large saucepan with a little cold water, salt and pepper. Cook on a high heat for 2 to 3 minutes until the water stars to boil. Drain and place the chard in wads of kitchen paper or clean tea towels, pressing down hard to drain the liquid out.

Heat the butter in a large frying pan and add the mushroom slices, seasoning with salt and pepper. Add the garlic, thyme and parsley. When the mushrooms start to caramelize in the hot butter, check the seasoning, then remove from the heat and set aside.

Grate the goat's cheese and combine three quarters of it with the eggs, ricotta, cream, nutmeg and lemon zest in a large bowl. Reserve the remaining cheese for the topping.

Spread a third of the ricotta mixture over the bottom of a large 28cm x 22cm ovenproof dish. Place half the chard on top and then a layer of the lasagne sheets. Put another third of the ricotta mixture on top, then layer with half the herby mushrooms.

Add the rest of the chard and then the remaining lasagne sheets. Spread the rest of the mushrooms on top, along with a final layer of ricotta sauce. Sprinkle the top with the remaining goat's cheese.

Bake in the oven for 30 to 40 minutes until golden brown on top, bubbling and ready to serve.

Breda's Cauliflower Cheese

Every week for as long as William can remember, his mother, Breda, has made this recipe. It is about as classic a cauliflower cheese as it gets, and all the more wonderful for that very fact – when something is this good it would be a crime to interfere with it!

SERVES 4 AS A SIDE DISH

- 1 large cauliflower
- sea salt and freshly ground black pepper
- 150g mature Irish Cheddar cheese
- 50g Parmesan cheese
- 1 small carrot
- 1 small onion
- 50g butter
- 50g cream flour
- 700ml milk
- 3 peppercorns
- 2 sprigs of fresh thyme
- a small bunch of fresh flat-leaf parsley
- 2 teaspoons Dijon mustard
- freshly grated nutmeg (optional)
- ground mace, to finish

METHOD

Preheat the oven to 200°C fan/gas 7.

Remove the thick base stalk from the cauliflower and discard, then break the cauliflower into florets. Steam the florets until tender. Season lightly with salt and place in an ovenproof dish. Grate the Cheddar and the Parmesan, keeping them separate.

Next make the béchamel sauce. Peel and chop the carrot, then peel and slice the onion. Make a roux by melting the butter in a small saucepan and adding the flour, stirring with a wooden spoon until thickened but not burned. Set aside.

Put the milk into a medium-sized saucepan with the carrot, onion, peppercorns, thyme and parsley. Bring to the boil, then simmer for 5 minutes.

Strain the milk into a jug, removing all the vegetables, herbs and peppercorns. Pour the milk slowly back into the saucepan with the roux and bring to the boil again, thoroughly whisking in the roux until thickened. Take off the heat and stir in the mustard, some salt and pepper, and a little nutmeg if desired.

Add the grated Cheddar to the béchamel while still hot, stirring gently until it is melted and combined. Check the seasoning and pour the sauce over the cauliflower florets.

Sprinkle the Parmesan on top and bake in the oven for 40 minutes until bubbling and golden. Sprinkle a little ground mace on top before serving.

FISH

Pan-fried Hake with Candy Beetroot and Orange Salad

Not only is this dish simple and delicious, but the pinks, oranges and yellows of the salad make it very beautiful. Because of its subtle fresh flavour and versatility, hake is William's favourite white fish to cook with.

SERVES 4

FOR THE SALAD:

- 4 medium-sized candy beetroots
- juice of 1 lemon and zest of ½ a lemon
- juice of ½ an orange
- sea salt and freshly ground black pepper
- 4 medium-sized oranges

FOR THE HAKE:

- 4 hake fillets, skin on (roughly 175g each)
- 1 tablespoon olive oil
- juice of ½ a lemon

TO GARNISH:

- 15g fresh flat-leaf parsley
- pink peppercorns, whole or lightly crushed, to taste

METHOD

First, make the salad. Slice the beetroots as thinly as possible into almost transparent rounds. In a shallow bowl, combine the slices with the lemon juice and zest, the orange juice and a pinch of salt and pepper.

Leave in the fridge for at least 30 minutes to marinate thoroughly and absorb the flavours. The beetroot should soften in this time but should retain a little crunch.

Peel the oranges and slice thinly into rounds, assembling them on a large platter with the marinated slices of candy beetroot. Spoon over a little of the marinating juices and season again with some salt and pepper.

Season your hake fillets with salt and pepper. Heat the olive oil in a frying pan and place the hake in skin side down, cooking them for around 3 minutes until the skin starts to crisp.

Turn them over carefully and cook for a further 3 or 4 minutes until they are cooked through but not overdone. Arrange the hake fillets on top of the beetroot and orange slices, squeeze the lemon juice over and sprinkle with parsley and pink peppercorns.

Slow-roasted Salmon with Blood Orange, Lemon, Fennel and Parsley

Blood orange may seem a surprising ingredient to pair with salmon, but it really enhances the subtle flavours of the dish and makes everything more zingy, fresh and vibrant.

SERVES 2

· 1 fennel bulb

· 2 lemons

· sea salt and freshly ground black pepper

· 1 blood orange

· 30g fresh flat-leaf parsley

· 2 salmon fillets, skin on (about 300g)

· olive oil

· a couple of sprigs of fresh dill to taste

METHOD

Preheat the oven to 150°C fan/gas 3.

Slice the fennel as thinly as possible and arrange on a plate. Squeeze the juice of half a lemon over the slices and sprinkle with salt. Carefully peel the blood orange and slice the flesh into thin rounds, arranging them on the plate with the fennel.

Pick and chop the parsley leaves and sprinkle half on top of the fennel and blood orange. Cover with cling film and leave in the fridge to marinate while you cook the salmon.

Season the salmon fillets with salt and pepper. Place skin side down in a small baking dish and squeeze the juice of half a lemon over the salmon. Slice the remaining lemon into thin rounds and arrange around and on top of the fish. Sprinkle with the remaining parsley and drizzle with olive oil.

Bake in the oven for 25 to 30 minutes until the salmon is slightly opaque. Place the salmon on top of the plated fennel and blood orange, scatter with the dill and serve.

Breda's Fish Pie

Fish pie on a Friday evokes strong memories of growing up in Currabinny. William's mum, Breda, would make it, and all the family looked forward to the smells from the stove, the fogged-up windows and taking turns to mash the buttery potato until it was smooth and velvety. Delicious smoky fish with a crusty potato topping – it was like a warm hug at the end of a long week.

SERVES 4–6

- 1 large onion
- 10 cloves
- 450ml milk
- 300ml double cream
- 3 sprigs of fresh thyme
- a small bunch of fresh flat-leaf parsley, plus extra to garnish
- 1 bay leaf
- 6 black peppercorns
- 750g good white fish fillets, such as cod or hake, skin on
- 250g smoked haddock, skin on
- 1 medium-sized leek
- 250g butter, plus extra for the leek
- rapeseed oil
- 4 medium organic eggs, plus 1 egg yolk
- 50g cream flour
- 1¼kg floury potatoes, such as Maris Piper
- sea salt and freshly ground black pepper
- 100g grated Irish Cheddar cheese

METHOD

Peel the onion, cut it in half and stud with the cloves. Put it in a large, heavy-based saucepan with the milk, cream, herbs and peppercorns. Add the fish fillets, bring to the boil gently and simmer uncovered for around 6 minutes.

Remove from the heat, pop the lid on and leave for a further 2 or 3 minutes, until cooked through.

Remove the fish when cool enough to handle, keeping the poaching liquid in the pan. Slip the skins off gently while removing any bones you might see, then flake the fish into large pieces.

Meanwhile, remove the green part of the leek (keep aside for stocks and soups), then wash the white part and thickly slice. Put a little butter and rapeseed oil into a saucepan on a medium heat to melt, then add the leek. Cook for around 6 minutes, until softened.

Boil 4 eggs in another saucepan for 8 minutes, take off the heat, run under cold water and remove the shells.

Strain the fish poaching liquid and return to the pan on a low heat. Make a roux in a small saucepan with 50g of the butter and the flour, whisking them together to form a thick brown paste. Whisk this roux into the poaching liquid until it starts to thicken.

Continued on page 113

Put the flaked fish back in, along with the leeks. Slice the eggs into quarters or eighths and add to the liquid too. Place everything in a large casserole dish or ovenproof dish. Preheat the oven to 180°C fan/gas 6.

Peel the potatoes and boil in salted water until a knife or skewer goes easily through them. Drain and mash together with the rest of the butter and some salt and pepper. Leave to cool slightly before stirring in the egg yolk.

Spoon the mash over the fish, run the tines of a fork all over the surface and sprinkle with the grated Cheddar.

Bake in the oven for around 30 minutes, until golden brown and bubbling. Leave to settle after removing it from the oven, sprinkle with some chopped parsley and serve.

Barbecued Mackerel

Catching mackerel is a powerful Currabinny memory. William recalls long summer days, high tides, and the schools of mackerel that would herd millions of tiny sprat into shallower waters. Amateur fishermen would descend upon the piers, slipways and low cliff edges around Cork Harbour. Those with boats could get behind the schools of mackerel and would reap the easiest catches. By the end of the summer, the freezer in Currabinny would be filled to bursting point.

Although completely native to Irish waters, there is something exotic about the marbled and tiger-striped, blue, green and black bodies of mackerel. If you can get them fresh during the summer, their rich oily flesh can take centre stage as part of a delicious and easily prepared lunch or dinner.

SERVES 2–4

- 2 whole fresh mackerel or 4 fresh fillets, skin on
- olive oil
- sea salt and freshly ground black pepper
- 1 lemon
- 8–10 sprigs of fresh thyme

METHOD

You can of course buy mackerel fillets in your local fishmonger, prepared and ready to cook. If you do have whole fish though, it is quite straightforward to fillet them yourself, as you'll see below. Make sure you light your barbecue before you prepare the fillets, so that it has enough time to heat up.

Using a sharp filleting knife, make an incision behind both fins behind the head of the fish. Flip the fish on to its belly and cut the head off, straight through the backbone. Throw the head away or keep for a fish stock – you could even use them as bait to catch other fish. Slice down the backbone of the fish's body, dragging the knife as close to it as possible. Repeat this on the other side until both fillets are removed. Use tweezers to remove the pin-bones from the middle of each fillet. Rinse the fillets with cold water and pat dry with kitchen paper.

Continued on page 117

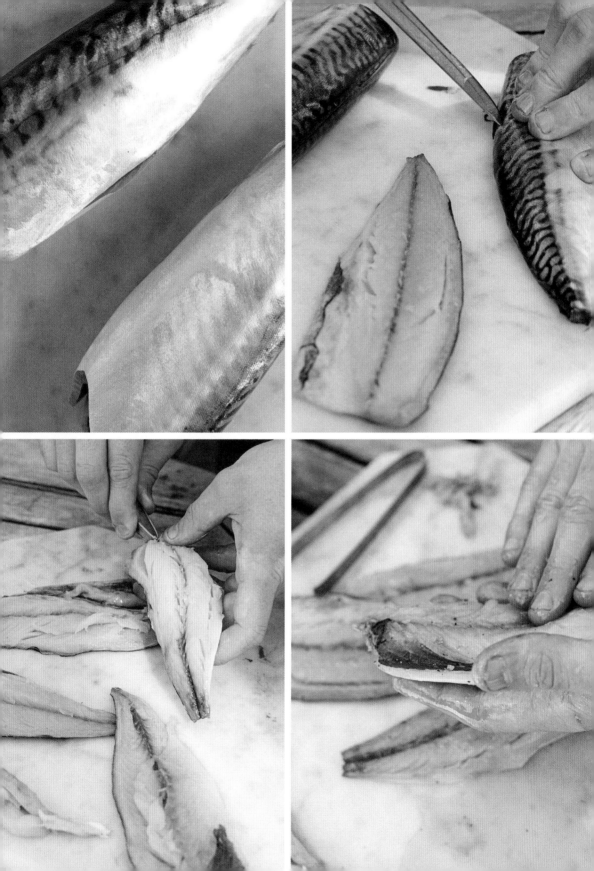

Rub some olive oil into the skin of the fish and season well with salt and pepper on both sides. Cut the lemon in half and slice one half into a few rounds. Squeeze the other half over the mackerel fillets.

Brush some olive oil over the hot grill (or a hot griddle pan) and arrange the sprigs of thyme as a sort of bed on the grill. Place the mackerel fillets skin side down on the thyme sprigs. The sprigs will likely burn and even catch fire, but this will all add to the smoky aroma you want the fish to absorb. After 3 to 4 minutes, turn the fillets over and cook for a further 3 to 4 minutes, until the flesh has turned grey-white. Garnish with the lemon rounds.

We like to serve this with a spicy cucumber pickle (see page 168) or, for a more substantial meal, a balsamic cucumber and Kalamata olive salad (see page 76) with some lemony Bretagne sauce (see page 178).

Salmon, Samphire, Broccoli and Cream Pappardelle

When William was growing up in Currabinny, one of his neighbours used to harvest samphire from the little cliffs that jut down from the forest and crumble into the sea. While he didn't think much of it then, he has grown to love this salty little weed, which is a perfect companion to fish.

SERVES 2

- 400g tenderstem broccoli
- 100g samphire
- 400g dried pappardelle pasta
- 2 tablespoons olive oil
- 350g salmon fillets, skin removed
- sea salt and freshly ground black pepper
- 150ml cream
- zest of 1 lemon
- 15g fresh flat-leaf parsley, leaves picked and chopped

METHOD

Bring some salted water to the boil in a small saucepan, add the broccoli and samphire and simmer for 2 minutes. Drain well, rinse with cold water and set aside.

In another, larger pan, bring some well-salted water to the boil and add the pasta. Simmer for 8 to 10 minutes until al dente. Drain and return to the pan, stir through 1 tablespoon of olive oil and set aside.

Cut the salmon into large pieces and season with salt and pepper. Heat the other tablespoon of oil in a large frying pan and add the salmon, together with the broccoli and samphire. Cook for around 1 minute before adding the cream.

Bring the cream to a simmer, then add the lemon zest, chopped parsley, and salt and pepper to taste. Make sure the salmon has been cooked all the way through before removing from the heat. Stir the pasta through the sauce and serve.

Salmon with Baby Potatoes, Capers and Garlic, Lemon and Parsley Butter

This is such a classic dish! It celebrates the purity of simple ingredients and is full of flavours that work together beautifully. In the summer use new-season baby potatoes, as they will be in abundance and at their very best.

SERVES 2

- 2 salmon fillets, skin on (about 150g each)
- sea salt and freshly ground black pepper
- 2 tablespoons olive oil
- 600g new potatoes
- 50g garlic, lemon and parsley butter (see page 173)
- 30g fresh flat-leaf parsley
- 2 tablespoons capers

METHOD

Preheat your oven to 150°C fan/gas 3.

Season the salmon fillets with salt and pepper. Drizzle the olive oil into a small baking dish and add the fillets skin side down. Bake in the oven for 25 to 30 minutes until the salmon is opaque and tender in the middle.

Meanwhile, put the new potatoes into a large pot of salted water and bring to the boil. Simmer for 20 to 25 minutes until just tender. Drain the potatoes well and add the garlic, lemon and parsley butter, coating thoroughly.

Pick and chop the parsley leaves and sprinkle, along with the capers, over the buttery new potatoes. Divide between two plates and top with the salmon fillets.

Smoked Rainbow Trout with Fennel, Goat's Cheese, Pink Peppercorns and Dill

Delicious flakes of pink trout and the luxury of soft goat's cheese make for surprisingly hearty eating. When making this, we like to use the very best ingredients: smoked trout from Goatsbridge Trout Farm in Kilkenny and goat's cheese from Ardsallagh Goat Farm in Cork – both delicious prize-winning Irish products and widely available.

SERVES 2-4

- 15g fresh dill
- 2 medium-sized fennel bulbs
- juice of ½ a lemon
- sea salt and freshly ground black pepper
- 1 tablespoon rapeseed oil
- 300g smoked rainbow trout
- 165g soft goat's cheese, such as Ardsallagh
- 2 teaspoons pink peppercorns

METHOD

Chop the dill. Slice the fennel as thinly as possible and arrange on a large plate. Squeeze the lemon juice over, sprinkle with salt, pepper and the chopped dill, and drizzle with the rapeseed oil.

Cover the plate with cling film and leave to marinate in the fridge for 20 to 30 minutes – the fennel should soften slightly as the acidic lemon juice 'cooks' it.

When the fennel has marinated, flake the smoked rainbow trout over it, add the goat's cheese in dollops all around the plate and sprinkle with the pink peppercorns. Simple, fresh and delicious, this is best served with hunks of decent bread to mop up the flavours.

Asparagus and Smoked Rainbow Trout with a Herb Sauce

This recipe is extremely simple, tasty and light. If you make the garlic, lemon and parsley butter for the ciabattas very heavy on the garlic, it plays well with the greenness of the asparagus and the herb sauce. This is perfect for a hot day when all you want is to be outside with a plate of something delicious and light on your lap!

SERVES 4

- 500g super-fine asparagus, untrimmed if young
- 1 large ciabatta loaf
- 75g garlic, lemon and parsley butter (see page 173)
- 4 smoked rainbow trout fillets
- 1 tablespoon of capers

FOR THE SAUCE:

- a good handful of fresh basil leaves
- a small bunch of fresh mint, leaves picked
- a good handful of fresh flat-leaf parsley leaves
- 4–5 anchovy fillets, drained
- 2 teaspoons Dijon mustard
- 4 tablespoons olive oil
- juice of ½ a lemon

METHOD

Blitz all the ingredients for the sauce in a food processor until smooth.

Cook the asparagus in a small pan with a splash of water until tender but still with a crunch – this should take around 2 minutes.

Slice the ciabatta thickly and spread generously with the garlic, lemon and parsley butter. Toast under a grill until it turns golden and the butter has melted and soaked through the bread.

Divide the slices of toast between four plates, top with some of the asparagus spears and flake a trout fillet over each then drizzle with the sauce and scatter the capers on top.

MEAT

Roast Chicken with Harissa Butter

A roast chicken dinner should be special, like it was in our grannies' time. When people you love are gathered around the table, a plump roast chicken is the most comforting of dishes. This is one of our favourite ways to prepare it. Anointing the bird generously with harissa butter keeps it moist and gives the flesh a subtle heat and fragrance.

SERVES 4–6

- 100g butter, at room temperature
- 2 teaspoons harissa (see page 165)
- 1 large organic chicken (about 1.5kg)
- sea salt and freshly ground black pepper
- 1 lemon
- 6 cloves of garlic, unpeeled
- 5 or 6 sprigs of fresh thyme

METHOD

Preheat the oven to 200°C fan/gas 7.

Make the harissa butter by mashing the butter in a bowl with the harissa until well combined.

Rub the chicken all over with the harissa butter, making sure you coat all of the skin, including the legs and wings. Use a knife to separate the skin from the flesh and rub some harissa butter under there as well. Season the chicken inside and out with salt and pepper.

Put the lemon, pierced several times with a knife, inside the chicken, together with 2 cloves of garlic and 2 sprigs of thyme. Place the chicken in a large roasting tin with the remaining thyme and garlic cloves scattered around it.

Put into the oven and cook for around 1 hour 20 minutes or until the juices run clear – the cooking time will depend on the size of the chicken. The skin might start to burn, so keep an eye on it and cover with tinfoil if necessary.

Remove from the oven and place on a large wooden board for carving. Here we've served it on a bed of herby couscous, but it would be equally good with roast potatoes and your favourite vegetables.

Penne Pasta with Ham, Cabbage, Wild Garlic Pesto and Pickled Walnut

This is another variation – an elevation, we go so far as to say! – of bacon and cabbage. Leftover ham is one of the most useful things you can have in your fridge. It's unbeatable here paired with its traditional companion – cabbage – and a garlicky pesto. Wild garlic pops up everywhere in early spring; make a big batch of this pesto when it's in season and you'll use it year round.

SERVES 2

- 200g penne pasta
- 1 tablespoon butter
- olive oil
- 1 savoy cabbage, shredded
- 100g cooked ham, or speck, prosciutto or pancetta
- 1 pickled walnut, sliced
- grated Parmesan cheese, to serve

FOR THE PESTO:

- 75g wild garlic, stalks removed
- 30g fresh flat-leaf parsley, stalks removed
- juice of ½ a lemon
- 80ml rapeseed oil, plus extra to seal the jar
- 30g Parmesan cheese, grated
- 30g walnuts
- sea salt and freshly ground black pepper, to taste

METHOD

Put the ingredients for the pesto into a food processor and blitz to a smooth paste. Decant into a sterilized jar and pour a little rapeseed oil over the top to seal. Refrigerate until needed (it will keep this way for 2 weeks).

Bring a large pot of salted water to the boil, add the penne and cook according to the packet instructions.

Meanwhile, put the butter and a drop of olive oil into a large, heavy-based frying pan on a medium heat and add the shredded cabbage. Season with a little salt and pepper. Cook the cabbage for 3 to 4 minutes until wilted,* then tear in the ham and cook for a further 2 minutes. Add a little of the pasta water if it looks dry.

Add 2 tablespoons of the wild garlic pesto and stir to combine, then cook for a further 2 to 3 minutes. When the pasta is cooked, drain in a colander and add to the pan, stirring the sauce into the pasta until it is all well coated. Serve with a few slices of pickled walnut on top, and offer some extra grated Parmesan.

*We would usually cook the cabbage so that it's softer and less crisp than the cabbage in the photograph. You can cook it to taste.

Ham in Juniper and Apple Juice

While there is nothing quite like a great boiled him, sometimes it can be a bit salty. A delicious solution is to cook it in a good cloudy apple juice. The mellow sweetness of the juice balances the saltiness of the meat beautifully.

SERVES 4–6

- 2kg boneless ham or gammon
- 2 litres cloudy apple juice
- 1 leek
- 1 stick of celery
- 1 carrot
- 12 juniper berries
- 12 black peppercorns
- a large bunch of fresh flat-leaf parsley
- 2 bay leaves

METHOD

Place the ham in a large pot and fill with cold water. Bring the water to boil, then take off the heat, drain the water and rinse the ham. Return the ham to the pot and pour in the apple juice, bringing it slowly to the boil.

Meanwhile, wash and trim the leek and cut it in half. Cut the celery stick in half too, and cut the carrot into large chunks. Add it all to the pot. Crush the juniper berries and peppercorns lightly with a knife and add these, along with the parsley (stems and all) and bay leaves.

When the apple juice has come to the boil, turn the heat down to a gentle simmer and scoop off any scum that has formed on the top.

Put a lid askew on the pot and leave to simmer for 2 hours, then check the ham to see if it is cooked through – to do this, remove it from the cooking liquid, pierce it with a knife and check if the juices are running clear.

Once it's ready, leave the ham to cool slightly in the cooking liquor for up to 20 minutes before carving. Lift out the ham, cut into thick slices and drizzle a little of the cooking liquor over the top (discarding the vegetables). This will keep the ham lovely and moist.

We like to serve this with some mustard parsnip mash (see page 158) and some fried apple and sage (see page 179).

Steak Sandwich with Fried Onions, Cashel Blue Cheese and Mushroom Ketchup

Living in the city, maybe juggling lots of daily commitments or working shifts, trying to grab dinner when running out the door again for work or meetings . . . this is the reality of life for many of us nowadays. This is William's favourite 'grab and go' meal. You can put it together super-quickly to eat in the back of a taxi on the way to your destination – but ask nicely before you tuck in!

SERVES 2

· 1 clove of garlic

· 1 medium-sized onion

· a handful of fresh flat-leaf parsley leaves

· 2 medium-sized striploin steaks

· sea salt and freshly ground black pepper

· olive oil

· 1 baguette, cut into two pieces

· 2 teaspoons Dijon mustard

· mushroom ketchup (see page 174)

· 50g Cashel Blue cheese

METHOD

Peel the garlic and onion and slice both thinly. Roughly chop the parsley. Place a griddle pan or frying pan on a medium heat and season the steaks with salt and pepper. When the pan is hot, cook the steaks in a little olive oil for 2 to 3 minutes on each side. Transfer to a board to rest for 5 minutes.

Meanwhile, put the sliced onion and a little more oil into the pan and cook for around 8 to 10 minutes until the onion is brown and softened. Add the sliced garlic and cook for another minute or so. Stir the parsley into the onion and garlic and take off the heat.

Open up the baguettes and spread a little mustard on one side of each and a little mushroom ketchup on the other. Cut the steaks into thick pieces and place inside the baguette. Crumble the cheese on top, then add the onions and sandwich together. Serve immediately.

Lamb Steak Sandwich with Garlic, Lemon and Parsley Butter and Wicklow Bán Brie

Imagine: molten cheese, juicy lamb, the crunch of sourdough bread, garlicky butter running down your fingers … this sandwich is pure indulgence!

SERVES 2

- 2 boneless lamb steaks
- sea salt and freshly ground black pepper
- 4 medium-sized chestnut mushrooms
- 2 tablespoons garlic, lemon and parsley butter (see page 173)
- olive oil
- 1 large sourdough baguette
- 2 tablespoons mayonnaise
- 4 thick slices of Wicklow Bán Brie or any good young Brie

METHOD

Preheat your grill. Season the lamb steaks liberally on both sides with salt and pepper. Wipe the mushrooms and slice thinly. Put the garlic, lemon and parsley butter and a little olive oil into a large frying pan on a high heat.

When the butter is bubbling, add the steaks and reduce the heat to medium. Cook for 2 minutes, then add the mushrooms and flip the lamb steaks over.

Cook for a further 4 minutes while spooning the butter over the top of the steaks and stirring the mushrooms occasionally.

Cut the baguette into two pieces widthways, then slice each piece in half lengthways. Put them under the hot grill for a couple of minutes until they turn golden.

Remove from the grill, then spread the mayonnaise on the top pieces of bread and drizzle some of the buttery juices from the frying pan over the bottom pieces, letting them soak into the bread.

Roughly chop the lamb steaks and place them on the bottom pieces of bread. Top with the mushrooms, then the slices of Brie. Put the top pieces of bread on and eat immediately, letting the juices run down your chin!

Turkey Burgers with Chanterelles and Gruyère

It's hard to make a case for turkey when you can just as easily have chicken – except in the case of this burger. Here, turkey – which can be dry and bland – is made juicy with some added bacon and gains depth of flavour from the Worcester sauce, saltiness from the Parmesan and a great aroma from the thyme and lemon zest. Topped with melted Gruyère, woody chanterelles and a little mayonnaise, and sandwiched between fluffy brioche buns, it is the ultimate burger.

SERVES 4

- 2 shallots
- 25g butter, plus extra to fry the shallots
- 450g lean turkey mince
- 150g streaky bacon, finely chopped
- 1 medium organic egg
- 30g breadcrumbs (made from slightly stale bread)
- 1 tablespoon fresh thyme leaves
- 1 tablespoon Worcester sauce
- 2 teaspoons lemon zest
- 2 tablespoons grated Parmesan cheese
- a good pinch of sea salt and freshly ground black pepper
- 200g chanterelle mushrooms
- 1 tablespoon chopped fresh flat-leaf parsley leaves
- olive oil
- 4 thin slices of Gruyère cheese
- 4 brioche buns
- mayonnaise
- a handful of mixed leaves, such as rocket, watercress, baby chard

METHOD

Peel and dice the shallots, then sauté in a frying pan with a little butter until softened. Put into a large mixing bowl with the turkey mince, bacon, egg, breadcrumbs, thyme, Worcester sauce, lemon zest and Parmesan. Season well with salt and pepper and mix thoroughly.

Form 4 equal-sized burgers with your hands and place on a plate in the fridge for 30 minutes.

Preheat your grill.

Put 25g of butter into a large pan on a medium-high heat, add the chanterelles and cook for around 5 minutes until soft. Add the parsley and season with salt and pepper. Transfer to a plate and drizzle over a little olive oil.

Fry the burgers in the pan over a medium heat, cooking for around 5 minutes on each side or until cooked through. Place a slice of Gruyère on top of each burger for the final 2 or 3 minutes of cooking.

Split the brioche buns and toast under the hot grill, then spread mayonnaise on both sides and add some salad leaves. Place a cheesy burger on the bottom half of each, load with the chanterelles and put the top piece of brioche on. Serve immediately.

Ferryhouse Cottage Pie

When William was growing up, cottage pie was a favourite way to use up the leftover beef from the Sunday roast. On the Monday the cold meat went through a mincer, was added to gravy, topped with potato mash and baked in the oven. Delicious! This recipe is our more up-to-date version made from raw minced beef, and is sure to become a comforting favourite.

The recipe is named in honour of William's home in Currabinny (left) – the house is called Ferryhouse because in olden times it was the home of the man who ran the ferry across the harbour from Currabinny to Crosshaven.

SERVES 4–6

- 1 large onion
- 2 medium-sized carrots
- 1 large stick of celery
- 500g lean minced beef
- sea salt and freshly ground black pepper
- 45g cream flour
- 200g butter
- 40ml Worcester sauce
- 750ml chicken stock
- 4 sprigs of fresh thyme
- a small bunch of fresh flat-leaf parsley, leaves picked and chopped
- cooked chard or spinach (optional)
- 1.2kg floury potatoes, such as Maris Piper
- 150ml milk
- 50g Irish Cheddar cheese, grated
- 50g Parmesan cheese, grated

METHOD

Peel and chop the onion and carrots. Finely chop the celery. Fry the mince in a large frying pan until brown and add the trio of onion, carrots and celery. Cook until the vegetables have softened, and season everything well with salt and pepper.

Add the flour, 50g of the butter, and the Worcester sauce, and cook for a further minute.

Heat the chicken stock in a saucepan and add to the frying pan, then bring to the boil and reduce to a simmer for 5 minutes. Add the thyme and parsley, then check the seasoning for salt and pepper.

Everything should have thickened nicely at this point. Transfer to a large casserole or ovenproof dish. For an extra dimension, you could layer some cooked chard or spinach on top.

Preheat the oven to 180°C fan/gas 6. Peel and chop the potatoes. Boil them in salted water until cooked through, then drain and mash together with the remaining butter and the milk.

Season the mash and scoop on top of the meat sauce, spreading to cover all the meat. Sprinkle with the grated Cheddar and Parmesan, then bake in the oven for 25 to 30 minutes until golden and bubbling.

Fried Cabbage and Ham Sandwich

This recipe reinvents the traditional bacon and cabbage dinner. Forget about over-boiled, greasy meat and veg. In this recipe, cabbage and ham are fried in garlicky, lemony butter. Then a crusty baguette soaks up the pan juices before being stuffed with the fried ingredients. You may want to eat straight from the pan, rather than bothering with a plate – we totally understand!

SERVES 1

- 2 tablespoons garlic, lemon and parsley butter (see page 173)

- olive oil

- a good handful of green or York cabbage

- 6 rough slices of cooked ham, or charcuterie ham such as speck, prosciutto or capicola

- a hunk of good-quality French baguette, cut in half

METHOD

In a large frying pan on a medium heat, melt the garlic, lemon and parsley butter with a drop of olive oil.

Shred the cabbage thinly and add to the pan, softening it for 2 or 3 minutes (you can wilt it more than in the photograph). Add the ham and cook for a further minute. Push the contents to one side and place the pieces of bread on the hot pan, allowing them to soak up the hot garlicky butter.

Spoon the ham and cabbage on to the bottom piece of baguette, put the top on and eat immediately.

Pappardelle with Speck, Ricotta, Beetroot Tops and Walnuts

This recipe came about when William brought home a big bunch of mucky beetroots. The inky purple had spread into the veins of the beautiful leaves and he couldn't bear to throw them away. Beetroot tops can be harder work than other leaves (even kale), but spending a little time – cooking them down until the purple stalks become tender and sweet – will reward you with a feast of peppery greenness. You can of course use chard instead, which is a relative of beetroot.

SERVES 4

- 20 or so beetroot tops, or 20 or so chard leaves (stalks removed), roughly chopped
- 1 clove of garlic
- 15g fresh flat-leaf parsley
- 80g shelled walnuts
- 400g dried pappardelle pasta
- 2 tablespoons butter
- 100g speck, sliced thinly
- juice of ½ a lemon
- 1 tablespoon grated Parmesan cheese

METHOD

Bring a large pot of salted water to boil for the pasta. Wash the beetroot tops well in cold water and leave to drain in a colander. Peel and thinly slice the garlic clove, then roughly chop the parsley leaves and walnuts.

Add the pasta to the pot and cook for 7 to 10 minutes until al dente. While the pasta is cooking, heat the butter in a saucepan and add the sliced garlic. When the garlic starts to turn golden and fragrant, add the beetroot tops, wilting them in the butter.

Next add the speck and stir through the pan for around 1 minute before adding the lemon juice and Parmesan.

Drain the pasta and add it to the pan, then take the pan off the heat and add some salt and pepper to taste. Stir through the chopped walnuts and parsley. Divide the pasta between four plates and garnish each one with several blobs of ricotta.

Sausage and Thyme Stuffing

Like many people in their twenties, we return to our parents for Christmas – you can't beat the traditional family Christmas! But in the weeks beforehand we like to gather with friends to have our own celebration and we all prepare something for the table. William came up with this sausage and thyme stuffing. It was meant to be just a small side dish; now it's a main in its own right. Such is its popularity that every year he has to bring a bigger dish, so he's very proud of it. A stuffing that outshines the turkey, the ham and the spiced beef – now that is a Christmas miracle!

SERVES 4 AS
A SIDE DISH

- 2 medium-sized onions
- 150g stale white bread
- sea salt and freshly ground black pepper
- 50g butter, melted, plus extra to fry the onions
- 50g cooked chestnuts, roughly chopped
- 800g good-quality sausage meat
- 2 tablespoons fresh thyme leaves

METHOD

Preheat the oven to 180°C fan/gas 6.

Peel and finely chop the onions. Blitz the bread with some salt and pepper in a food processor to make breadcrumbs. In a large bowl, mix the breadcrumbs, melted butter, chestnuts and sausage meat together.

Sauté the chopped onions until soft in a frying pan with a little butter. Leave to cool slightly and add to the sausage meat mixture. Stir through the thyme leaves and scoop the mixture into a ceramic baking dish.

Bake in the oven for 30 to 40 minutes, until golden brown on top.

SIDE DISHES

Gags's Potato Gratin

James's mum, Gags, used to call into his old workplace once
a week with a big dish of her potato gratin, still hot from the oven.
The whole office would go wild for it, and there would be a dash
to the kitchen to get plates and a spatula to divide and conquer.
It's rich and irresistible, and a guaranteed way to people's hearts!

SERVES 4–6

- Butter for greasing
- 110g strong
  Cheddar cheese
- 55g Parmesan cheese
- 55g cold butter
- 2 cloves of garlic
- 4 large or 7 medium
  potatoes
- 500ml fresh cream
- sea salt and freshly
  ground black pepper

METHOD

Preheat the oven to 190°C fan/gas 6 and lightly butter
a gratin dish.

Grate the two cheeses together, chop the cold butter into
small pieces, and peel and finely chop the garlic. Peel
and thinly slice the potatoes.

Put a layer of potatoes in the prepared dish and sprinkle
on some cheese and pieces of butter, continuing to layer
in this way until all the potato is used. Reserve some
cheese for the topping.

Mix the cream, garlic and some salt and pepper in
a jug and pour over the potatoes in the dish. Sprinkle
the remaining cheese on top, cover with tinfoil and bake
in the oven for 1 hour.

Remove the tinfoil and bake for about 15 minutes until
bubbling and nicely browned. Leave to set in the dish
for about 15 minutes before serving.

Colcannon with Curly Kale

Curly kale is perhaps the least attractive, toughest and most misunderstood of the kale or brassica varieties. It deserves more love, and here is a recipe that gives it the treatment it deserves: wilted down until tender and mixed with buttery mashed potatoes in this wonderful traditional dish.

SERVES 4–6

- 4–5 medium-sized floury potatoes, such as Red Rooster
- 2 leeks
- 100g butter, plus an extra knob to serve
- 200g curly kale
- a handful of chopped wild garlic (optional)
- 250ml milk
- 175ml double cream
- sea salt and freshly ground black pepper
- 2 spring onions, sliced thinly

METHOD

Peel the potatoes, wash and trim the leeks and chop both roughly, keeping them separate. Boil the potatoes in a large pot of salted water for 15 to 20 minutes until cooked through. Remove and drain.

In a large saucepan, heat 100g of butter and add the leeks. Sauté gently for around 10 minutes until softened. Meanwhile, remove the stalks from the curly kale and discard, then roughly chop the leaves. Add the wild garlic to the pan if using, then add the chopped kale and cook until wilted.

Pour in the milk and cream and bring to a simmer. Tip in the cooked potatoes and season with salt and pepper. Mash the mixture with a potato masher until smooth. Stir through an extra knob of butter for good measure, together with the spring onions, and transfer to a serving dish.

Colcannon with curly kale is shown on page 146

Ginger-braised Leeks

This is perfect at any time, but particularly as part of a winter dinner. Ginger is not only warm and aromatic, it's also good for you. Using it like this makes for a really comforting side dish.

SERVES 2–4

- 2 medium-sized leeks
- 1 thumb-sized piece of fresh ginger
- 1 tablespoon rapeseed oil
- 25g butter
- 4–5 sprigs of fresh thyme
- juice of ½ a lemon
- 80ml white wine
- sea salt and freshly ground black pepper

METHOD

Preheat the oven to 180°C fan/gas 6.

Remove the green part of the leeks (keep aside for stocks and soups), then wash the white part and chop into thickish rounds. Peel and grate the ginger and set aside.

Heat the rapeseed oil and butter in a heavy-based frying pan until sizzling. Add the leeks, stirring to coat in the oil and butter. Gently soften over a medium-low heat, being careful to keep the rounds intact.

Transfer the leek rounds to a roasting pan, filling the bottom in a single layer. Cover with the ginger, thyme and lemon juice, and pour the wine over everything. Drizzle with oil if desired. Season with salt and pepper.

Roast in the oven for 25 to 30 minutes until the edges of the leeks start to brown and almost all of the liquid has evaporated.

Mushroom à la Crème

Much as William loves fresh local ingredients, he has a love–hate relationship with mushrooms. On the positive side, there are many varieties to choose from and the fact you can forage for them However, they can be pungent and overpowering when left to their own devices. This recipe – using butter, herbs, cream and lemon juice – treats mushrooms with respect and brings out their natural earthy nuttiness. It's a truly delicious side dish.

SERVES 2–4

- 225g chestnut mushrooms (or a mix of chestnut and chanterelles)
- 1 shallot
- 15g fresh flat-leaf parsley
- 5 fresh chives
- 50g butter
- sea salt and freshly ground black pepper
- olive oil
- 125ml cream
- juice of ½ a small lemon

METHOD

Wipe and thinly slice the mushrooms. If using chanterelles, you can leave them whole. Peel and finely dice the shallot, and chop the parsley leaves and chives. Place a large, heavy-based saucepan on a medium heat and put the butter into the pan. When melted, add the shallot and cook for 5 to 10 minutes until softened.

Season the mushrooms well with salt and pepper. Add them to the pan and stir through the shallot and butter. Add a little drizzle of olive oil and increase the heat. Cook for around 10 minutes until the mushrooms are soft, brown and smelling nutty.

Pour in the cream and allow to bubble, then reduce the heat and add the lemon juice, parsley and chives, stirring them through. Serve immediately.

Buttery Purple Carrots

It's worth looking out for purple carrots. Their peppery sweetness is a wonderful match for roast pork or game birds like pheasant or duck. But don't worry if you can't find the purple variety – the regular orange ones are also delicious when prepared this way!

SERVES 4

- 6 purple carrots (or a mix of purple and orange)
- 1 tablespoon butter
- olive oil
- 1 tablespoon caster sugar
- 50ml water
- sea salt and freshly ground black pepper
- 1 tablespoon roughly chopped fresh flat-leaf parsley leaves

METHOD

Wash the carrots and thickly slice them at an angle. Heat the butter and a drizzle of olive oil in a large, heavy-based saucepan until bubbling. Add the sugar and water and stir for a moment. Tip in the slices of carrot and stir to coat, seasoning with salt and pepper.

Put a lid slightly askew on the saucepan and cook on a medium-high heat for 10 minutes. Remove the lid, throw in the parsley and cook for another 5 minutes or so, stirring occasionally. It is ready when the liquid has mostly evaporated, leaving the carrots coated in a syrupy, buttery sauce.

Mustard Parsnip Mash

A satisfying combination of sweet parsnip and warming Dijon mustard, this is a perfect accompaniment to ham, pork, game and other wintry, hearty meats.

SERVES 2–4

- 800g parsnips
- 80g butter
- a drizzle of rapeseed oil
- a pinch of sea salt and freshly ground black pepper
- 1 teaspoon lemon juice
- 1 tablespoon Dijon mustard

METHOD

Peel the parsnips and cut into small cubes. Melt the butter and rapeseed oil in a large pan on a medium heat. Add the parsnips and stir to coat all of the pieces with butter. Cook for 8 to 10 minutes until soft and sticking to the pan.

Reduce the heat to low and season with the salt, pepper and lemon juice. With a potato masher, crush the parsnips into a mash, adding a little more butter if needed. Stir the mustard through and serve.

Potato and Chive Cake

This potato cake is gentle and comforting and has subtle chive flavours. It works really well with most things and it's also very satisfying on its own. Throw in a bit of salad on the side and you have a perfect light lunch.

SERVES 4

- 800g large potatoes
- 3 onions
- a bunch of fresh chives
- 4 medium organic eggs
- sea salt and freshly ground black pepper
- 1 tablespoon olive oil

METHOD

Peel and grate the potatoes, then peel and slice the onions thinly. Chop the chives finely. In a medium-sized bowl, lightly beat the eggs and stir in the grated potato, onions and chives. Season with salt and pepper.

Heat the olive oil in a large frying pan and add the potato mixture, flatten with a spatula and cook over a gentle heat for around 8 minutes. Turn over carefully and cook for another 8 minutes.

Buttered Cabbage with Caraway or Fennel Seeds

Caraway and fennel seeds are both earthy and sweet. They add subtly different anise flavours to the cabbage – fennel is a simple flavour and well liked; caraway is more complex, earthy and aromatic and tends not to be quite as popular – so you can experiment to see which you prefer. We never blanch the cabbage beforehand as the butter, oil and heat of the pan combine to tenderize the thin shreds perfectly. This dish would go perfectly with the ham in juniper and apple juice on page 132.

SERVES 2–4

- ½ a savoy cabbage
- 75g butter
- rapeseed oil
- ½ teaspoon caraway seeds or 1 teaspoon fennel seeds
- sea salt and freshly ground black pepper

METHOD

Shred the cabbage into long thin ribbons. Melt the butter with a small drizzle of rapeseed oil in a medium, heavy-based pan. Add the cabbage and cook on a medium-high heat for 5 minutes until it is all wilted and well coated in the butter.

Add the caraway or fennel seeds and some salt and pepper, reduce the heat to medium and cook for a further 8 to 10 minutes, stirring continuously. You want the cabbage to brown slightly and become almost sticky and caramelized.

PRESERVES, DIPS & CONDIMENTS

Kale, Cashew and Wakame Pesto

Curly kale sometimes seems like the poor relation of leafy green vegetables. For years, people avoided it. Then, because it's so fabulously good for you, it became trendy and everyone pretended to enjoy it raw, covered in lemon juice – as if that was going to soften the tough leaves. In our opinion, kale is best eaten cooked, not raw – except in this recipe, where it's blitzed with oil, cheese, lemon juice and nuts to create a delicious peppery pesto that brims with goodness and flavour. The addition of wakame seaweed gives a lovely hint of the sea.

MAKES ABOUT 250G

- 2 cloves of garlic, peeled
- 60g curly kale, stalks removed
- 30g dried wakame, soaked in water and drained
- juice of 1 lemon
- 60g cashew nuts
- 80ml rapeseed oil
- 60g hard cheese such as Gruyère or Parmesan, or a hard mature sheep's cheese such as Cáis na Tíre or Cratloe Hills, grated

METHOD

Put all the ingredients into a food processor and whiz until well combined but still textured and chunky. Add more oil to loosen up the mixture if needed.

It will keep in the fridge for up to 2 weeks in a sterilized jar and is delicious stirred through pasta, dolloped on top of soups or spread on crackers.

The pesto is shown middle right in the picture

Beetroot and Seaweed Hummus

Hummus wasn't something we ate traditionally in Currabinny. But we grew beetroot in the garden. It was scrubbed hard, boiled, allowed to cool and then either pickled in spicy vinegar or sliced into a salad. Adding beetroot to hummus, with flakes of dillisk seaweed and some horseradish for a little background heat, gives an earthy, sweet, salty and decidedly Irish twist to this Middle Eastern delicacy.

MAKES ABOUT 800G

- 2 tablespoons finely chopped dillisk, plus extra flakes to garnish
- 200g beetroot, cooked and peeled
- 1 x 400g tin of chickpeas, drained
- juice of ½ a lemon
- 3 tablespoons tahini
- 2 teaspoons ground coriander
- 100ml rapeseed oil
- a handful of fresh flat-leaf parsley leaves, plus extra to garnish
- 1 clove of garlic, peeled
- sea salt and freshly ground black pepper, to taste
- 1 tablespoon horseradish (or more to taste)

METHOD

Put all of the ingredients into a food processor apart from the horseradish and the garnishes. Whiz until smooth and thick.

Scoop the mixture into a serving bowl and stir the horseradish through. Garnish with a few chopped parsley leaves and seaweed flakes.

The hummus is shown on top right in the picture on page 162

Harissa

Spices toasting in a dry pan, the scent of roses, the intense heat of red chillies … though harissa will transport you to foreign lands, it will also become a staple in your kitchen. Harissa is a North African chilli paste, but we use it for all kinds of things. Whether whipped into good Irish butter that's spread over a chicken for roasting (see page 128), or combined with oil and vinegar to make a lively salad dressing, it can make any number of dishes more luxurious and special.

MAKES 1 X 190ML JAR

- ½ teaspoon cumin seeds
- ½ teaspoon fennel or caraway seeds
- ½ teaspoon coriander seeds
- 5 small fresh red chillies
- 5 small dried chillies
- 1 clove of garlic, peeled
- 2 teaspoons Pedro Ximénez sherry vinegar
- 2 tablespoons rapeseed oil
- 2 teaspoons tomato purée
- a pinch of sea salt
- ½ teaspoon preserved lemon skin
- 1 teaspoon rose water
- ¼ teaspoon dried rose petals

METHOD

Toast the cumin, fennel/caraway and coriander seeds in a dry pan for a few minutes until a fragrant aroma rises up. Remove the stalks from the fresh chillies and if you don't like it too hot, slice them all in half and remove the seeds.

Blitz all the ingredients, including the toasted seeds, in a food processor until smooth and well combined.

Transfer into a small sterilized jar and refrigerate – it will keep for at least 2 weeks.

The harissa is shown on bottom right in the picture on page 162

Spicy Pickled Carrot

The mix of spices and textures in this pickle makes it rich and aromatic. It's best eaten a few days after pickling when the peppercorns have softened and the flavours have really intensified. Perfect on a flatbread with hummus and lamb or in a sandwich or salad.

MAKES ABOUT 650G

- 500g carrots
- 1 tablespoon rapeseed oil
- 1½ teaspoons cumin seeds
- 2 teaspoons mustard seeds
- ½ teaspoon fennel seeds
- 5 curry leaves
- 1 teaspoon black peppercorns
- 150ml apple cider vinegar

FOR THE PASTE:

- 2 teaspoons cumin seeds
- 2 fresh red chillies, finely chopped
- a pinch of sea salt
- 4 cloves of garlic, crushed
- 50g fresh ginger, peeled and chopped
- 100g soft brown sugar
- 3 tablespoons rapeseed oil

METHOD

First make the paste. Using a large pestle and mortar, grind all the ingredients for the paste together until smooth and pungent.

Peel and grate the carrots into a large bowl. Heat the oil in a large, heavy-based saucepan and add the cumin, mustard and fennel seeds, cooking for a few seconds until you hear the seeds start to pop. Add the curry leaves and peppercorns and cook for 2 minutes.

Add the spice paste next and cook for a further 2 minutes before adding the vinegar and bringing to a simmer. Add the carrots and stir well to coat. Cook for a further 15 minutes on a medium-low heat. Leave to cool before placing in sterilized jars. It will keep for several months in the fridge.

The pickled carrot is shown on the left in the picture on page 162

Spicy Cucumber Pickle

Adding a little chilli heat to cucumber seems to intensify its subtle and refreshing flavour. This is a gorgeous pickle that goes well with a slice of stout and treacle loaf (see page 38) or makes as a great accompaniment to a sandwich or salad.

MAKES 1 x 200ML JAR

- ½ a small fresh red chilli
- 2 cucumbers
- 60ml white wine vinegar
- 2 teaspoons sea salt
- 1 teaspoon caster sugar

METHOD

Scrape out the seeds from the chilli and chop as finely as possible. Slice the cucumbers as thinly as possible into rounds. Put these into a bowl together with the vinegar, salt and sugar. Cover with cling film and leave to marinate for at least 2 hours.

This keeps for several months at least if stored in a sterilized jar in a cool, dark place.

The cucumber pickle is shown at the top in the picture on page 162

Tahini Dressing

Combining the nuttiness of tahini with the bright zing of lemon, this creamy dressing is perfect drizzled over any combination of leaves, salad vegetables or roasted root vegetables.

MAKES 120ML

- juice of ½ a lemon
- 1 tablespoon honey
- 5 tablespoons tahini
- 2 tablespoons rapeseed oil
- 1 teaspoon sea salt
- 2 cloves of garlic, crushed
- freshly ground black pepper, to taste

METHOD

Put all the ingredients into a large bowl and whisk thoroughly to combine. It will keep for at least a month in the fridge in a sterilized jar.

Flavoured Butters

Butter makes everything taste better. In Ireland we are lucky to have the best butter in the world. This is something to be proud of and to celebrate – it's part of what we are, and our ancestors probably had it running through their veins. We now know that butter is a good fat, full of nutrients and vitamins, so we needn't be afraid of it. While butter on its own is great, adding flavours – such as garlic, onion, seaweed, herbs, honey, fruits, spices – can make it special.
At our markets we always have a good selection of flavoured butters …

· 2 small onions

· olive oil

· 125g butter, softened

· a pinch of sea salt

BURNT ONION BUTTER

Peel the onions. Cut one into dice and slice the other one finely. In a frying pan on a medium-low heat, cook the diced onion in a little olive oil for around 20 minutes, until golden brown and starting to stick to the pan. Add more oil or a splash of water to the pan if the onion starts to become too dry or burn. Leave to cool, and preheat your grill.

Lay out the sliced onion on some baking parchment on a baking tray, put under the hot grill and cook until completely dry, black and burnt beyond recognition. Remove from the grill, tip the charred onion into a pestle and mortar, and grind to a fine black powder.

In a bowl, mix the butter, cooled caramelized onion and salt until well combined. Mould into a ramekin and, using a brush, gently dust the top with the burnt onion dust until completely covered. Place in the fridge to harden. Take out and spread on everything.

Continued on page 173

ORANGE AND CINNAMON BUTTER

- ½ teaspoon ground cinnamon
- zest of 1 orange
- 125g butter, softened

Beat the cinnamon and most of the orange zest into the butter until well combined. Mould into a ramekin, cover with the remaining orange zest and refrigerate. Delicious slathered on toast or scones.

KOMBU BUTTER

- 10g dried kombu
- 125g butter, softened
- sea salt and freshly ground black pepper
- juice of ½ a lemon
- 1 clove of garlic, crushed

Break the kombu into small pieces and place in a cup of water for a few moments to soften. Remove from the water and dry on paper towels. Put the butter into a bowl and mix together with salt, pepper, the lemon juice, garlic and kombu until well combined. Transfer to a ramekin and chill in the fridge to set. Kombu butter is amazing on the seeded dillisk loaf from page 40. It is also perfect tossed into steamed samphire or green beans and served with fish.

HONEY AND REDCURRANT BUTTER

- 125g butter, softened
- 1 tablespoon honey
- 2 tablespoons fresh redcurrants

In a bowl, mix the butter with the honey, combining it well until smooth. Using a fork, incorporate the redcurrants into the honeyed butter trying to keep them whole. If they release their juice into the butter they won't mix well. Transfer the butter into a ramekin and refrigerate until set. Spread on pastries, bread or anything you desire.

GARLIC, LEMON AND PARSLEY BUTTER

- 10g fresh flat-leaf parsley
- 125g butter, softened
- sea salt and freshly ground black pepper
- juice of ½ a lemon
- 1 clove of garlic, crushed

Chop the parsley leaves finely. Place the butter in a bowl and mix together with some salt, pepper, the lemon juice, garlic and parsley until well combined. Transfer to a ramekin and chill in the fridge to set. This is probably the most versatile butter we make, as it works well on anything from pasta to steak and is also delicious spread generously on any type of bread.

Mushroom Ketchup

This is a deep, rich, woody alternative to traditional tomato ketchup. In fact, ketchup was first made with mushrooms instead of tomatoes, so technically this is a more traditional version! It is perfect for steak or anything that you would usually put tomato ketchup on.

MAKES ABOUT 350ML

- 600g chestnut mushrooms
- 2 tablespoons sea salt
- 25g dried porcini mushrooms
- 100ml sherry vinegar
- ¼ teaspoon freshly grated nutmeg
- 2 shallots, finely diced
- 1 thumb-sized piece of fresh ginger, peeled and sliced
- 1 bay leaf
- 1 teaspoon black peppercorns
- ½ teaspoon allspice berries

METHOD

You will need to start making this a week before you want to use it.

Wipe and slice the chestnut mushrooms and put into a large bowl with the salt. Cover with cling film and leave for 24 hours. Every so often, press down the mushrooms and stir with a wooden spoon until they start to release their juices and break up slightly.

Put the porcini mushrooms into 125ml of boiling water and leave to soak for an hour or so. Remove the porcini mushrooms and pour the water into a jug through a fine sieve to remove any grit.

Place the chestnut mushrooms along with any liquid they have released in a large pan with the vinegar, then add the porcini mushrooms along with their soaking water, the nutmeg and the shallots.

Put the ginger, bay leaf, peppercorns and allspice berries into a piece of muslin tied with string and place in the pan. Bring to the boil and then simmer gently, uncovered, for around 1½ hours. Stir the mixture regularly until it has started to thicken.

Discard the bag of spices, then transfer the mixture from the pot into a food processor and blitz until very smooth. You can also use a hand blender for this, but you may need to blitz the ingredients for longer to reach the right consistency.

Return the smooth sauce to the pan and bring to the boil, then simmer for 5 minutes. Pour into sterilized jars and leave to develop its flavour for around one week before using. It should keep unopened in a cool place for 3 months.

Walnut and Feta Dip

This is an impressive-tasting dip. Pairing walnuts with feta deepens and mellows the mix and balances the tanginess and sharpness of the cheese. Though it tastes complex, it couldn't be easier to make.

MAKES ABOUT 300G

- 120g walnuts, roughly chopped
- 2 tablespoons chopped fresh flat-leaf parsley leaves
- 150g feta cheese
- 1 clove of garlic
- 2 tablespoons rapeseed oil
- juice of ½ a lemon
- a little freshly ground black pepper
- a little smoked paprika and a drizzle of olive oil, to garnish

METHOD

Put 100g of the walnuts and 1 tablespoon of the parsley into a food processor, then add the rest of the ingredients except for the paprika and olive oil.

Blitz until smooth, then stir in the reserved walnuts and parsley. Place in a nice bowl and drizzle with a little olive oil and a small sprinkling of paprika. Great on toasted flatbreads.

Green Herb and Lemon Dressing

This is a super-bright, zingy dressing that is perfect for fresh garden leaves. The recipe makes a small quantity, but it is packed with flavour so it goes a long way.

MAKES 100ML

- 2 tablespoons fresh flat-leaf parsley leaves
- 2 tablespoons fresh chervil leaves
- 1 tablespoon fresh French tarragon leaves
- 1 teaspoon fresh marjoram leaves
- juice of 1 lemon
- 1 tablespoon capers
- 3 tablespoons rapeseed oil, plus extra if needed
- sea salt and freshly ground black pepper

METHOD

Combine all the ingredients in a food processor or blender and blitz until you have a bright green sauce. Add more rapeseed oil if needed – the consistency should be quite loose and runny.

Spring Onion Vinaigrette

William likes this bright, fresh vinaigrette on everything, especially his poached eggs in the morning!

SERVES 1

- 4 spring onions
- a pinch of sea salt and freshly ground black pepper
- juice of 1 lemon
- 1 tablespoon rapeseed oil

METHOD

Slice 3 of the spring onions thinly and place in a pestle and mortar with the salt and pepper. Grind to a rough paste and transfer to a small bowl with the lemon juice and oil. Whisk gently with a fork. Cut the remaining spring onion into small rounds and add to the bowl, stirring to combine. This is particularly good drizzled over poached eggs (see page 27).

Lime and Coriander Mayo

We love this version of mayonnaise – the lime juice gives it such a refreshing zing! Sadly, coriander isn't for everyone, so if it's not your thing just leave it out. This would be amazing in a halloumi burger or with some freshly grilled mackerel.

MAKES 320ML

- 15g fresh coriander
- 2 medium egg yolks
- 1 tablespoon white wine vinegar
- ¼ teaspoon Dijon mustard
- a pinch of sea salt
- 250ml sunflower oil
- juice of 1 lime

METHOD

Roughly chop the coriander leaves. In a large bowl, whisk the egg yolks together with the vinegar, mustard and salt. Slowly pour the oil into the bowl in a thin but steady stream while whisking vigorously. Be careful not to add the oil too fast or the mixture will curdle.

The mixture will quickly thicken until you are left with a nice pale yellow homemade mayonnaise. Stir in the lime juice and coriander, mixing until well combined. This keeps for 2 weeks in a sterilized jar in the fridge.

Bretagne Sauce

This is a Breton variation of a classic hollandaise sauce that's great with seafood and particularly good for oily fish like mackerel or kippers. It's also a bit easier to make than hollandaise.

MAKES ABOUT 200ML

- 2 medium egg yolks
- juice of ½ a lemon
- 1 teaspoon Dijon mustard
- 2 tablespoons white wine vinegar
- 1 tablespoon chopped fresh chervil or flat-leaf parsley leaves (or both)
- 55g butter

METHOD

Put the egg yolks, lemon juice, mustard, vinegar and herbs into a large bowl. Melt the butter in a small pan and slowly drizzle it into the egg yolk mixture, whisking vigorously to combine.

Continue to whisk until the sauce thickens and becomes silky smooth in texture. Be careful not to allow the mixture to split by adding the butter too quickly.

This sauce keeps for 3 to 4 days in the fridge.

Fried Apple and Sage

The sweetness of apples goes wonderfully with savoury dishes like pork, cold meats, and cheese and pickles. But these fried apples also work well when given a starring role – for instance, on top of a rye cracker or inside a wholemeal pitta.

SERVES 2–4 AS SIDE DISH, MORE ON CRACKERS

- 4 apples (preferably Cox's)
- 25g butter
- olive oil
- 12–20 fresh sage leaves
- 1 tablespoon fresh thyme leaves
- sea salt and freshly ground black pepper

METHOD

Core the apples, unpeeled, and cut into quarters. In a frying pan over a medium heat, melt the butter with a little olive oil. Add the apples, sage and thyme leaves, stirring to coat with the butter. Season with salt and pepper.

Keep turning in the frying pan for around 4 minutes, until the apples start to caramelize around the edges and the flesh is soft but not falling apart.

Leave to cool and decant to sterilized jars, then leave in a cool place until ready to serve. It will keep for up to a week.

This recipe is pictured overleaf

SWEET THINGS

Pear and Frangipane Tart

This is a classic recipe that everyone who goes to the Ballymaloe Cookery School will know and love. William's version makes the pastry extra short, because that's how we like it! And lacing your frangipane filling with a good slosh of kirsch brings out the subtle flavours of the pears and gives the tart more kick!

MAKES 8 SLICES

FOR THE SIMPLE
SHORTCRUST PASTRY:

- 240g cream flour, plus extra for dusting

- a pinch of sea salt

- 2 teaspoons caster sugar

- 180g cold butter

- 1 medium organic egg yolk

- 1–2 tablespoons chilled water

FOR THE POACHED PEARS:

- 1 litre water

- 4 Conference pears

- 1 vanilla pod

- 3 x 2cm pieces of lemon peel

- juice of 1 lemon

- 200g caster sugar

METHOD

Sift the flour for the pastry into a large bowl and add the salt and sugar. Cut the cold butter into cubes and rub into the flour with your fingers until the mixture resembles breadcrumbs.

Add the egg yolk and just enough of the water to bring the mixture together into a ball. We like it as short as possible, so don't worry if it's a little crumbly and hard to handle. Shape into a thick disc, cover in cling film and put in the fridge for 30 to 40 minutes.

Put the water for the poached pears on to boil in a large, heavy-based saucepan. Peel the pears and cut them in half, then remove the core with a melon baller or teaspoon. We like to keep the stalks intact if the pears still have them.

Split the vanilla pod, leaving it attached at the top, and add it to the pot of boiling water, together with the pears, lemon peel, lemon juice and sugar. Bring back to the boil, then reduce to a simmer.

Construct a cartouche by cutting a circle of baking parchment which perfectly covers the inside of your pan. Place it inside the pan, put a lid slightly askew over it and leave to simmer gently for 20 minutes.

Test the pears with a sharp knife – if it slides through them easily, they are done. Remove the pan from the heat and leave the pears to cool in their cooking liquid. When everything has cooled, remove the pears with a slotted spoon and drain on kitchen paper.

Continued on page 186

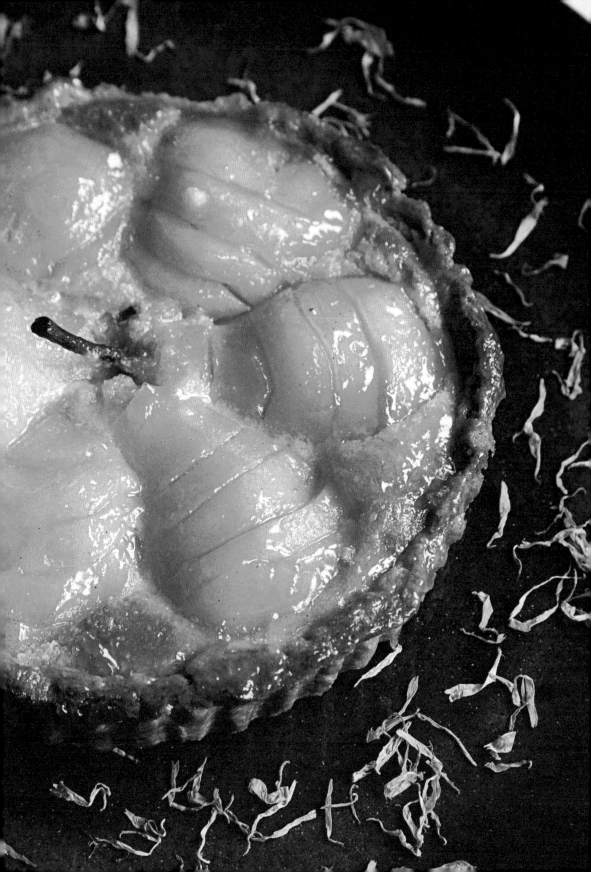

- 80g butter, softened
- 80g caster sugar
- 1 medium organic egg
- 100g ground almonds
- 1 tablespoon cream flour
- 1–3 tablespoons kirsch, to taste

FOR THE APRICOT GLAZE:

- 2 tablespoons apricot jam
- 2 teaspoons water

To make the frangipane, cream the butter and sugar together in a large bowl until smooth and pale.

Add the egg, beating vigorously to avoid the mixture splitting. Stir in the ground almonds and flour until well incorporated. Add the kirsch at the end – we use 3 tablespoons, which is quite strong, so try adding a tablespoon at a time and tasting the mixture as you go to get the flavour you like.

Preheat the oven to 180°C fan/gas 6.

Roll out your chilled pastry on a lightly floured surface to around 1cm thick. The pastry will be a little difficult to handle, but stick with it and you will be rewarded with the most mouth-watering crumbly crust. Carefully flip the pastry on to a 20cm fluted loose-bottomed tart tin – there will be breakages, cracks and gaps, but don't panic; just use the excess pastry to patch everything up. Press gently into the sides of the tin and leave a rim of about 1cm hanging over the edges.

Line the pastry case with baking parchment, fill with baking beans and place in the oven for 10 to 15 minutes, until golden. Remove from the oven, lift out the paper and beans, and leave to cool.

When cool, fill the case with the frangipane. Slice the poached pears from stalk to base in 1cm pieces, retaining their pear shape. Arrange the pieces in a tight circle on top of the frangipane, stalks facing inwards.

Bake in the oven for 20 minutes, then reduce the temperature to 160°C fan/gas 4 and bake for another 10 minutes until golden brown on top. Leave to cool slightly before removing from the tart tin.

Prepare the apricot glaze by warming the jam with the water over a low heat. Pass the mixture through a sieve to remove any lumps and brush over the top of the tart. Allow the tart to cool completely before serving.

Fresh Blueberry Pie with a Lemon Curd Cream

Blueberries tend to burst and fall apart when cooked, so cooks often add a load of sugar to compensate, which makes most blueberry pies tooth-achingly sweet. In our version you cook just a quarter of the blueberries in a syrupy sauce and then fold in the remaining fresh blueberries. This way the gorgeous sharp blueberry flavour remains the star of the show!

SERVES 8–10

FOR THE SHORTCRUST PASTRY:

- 240g cream flour
- a pinch of sea salt
- 2 teaspoons caster sugar
- 180g cold butter
- 1 medium organic egg
- 1–2 tablespoons chilled water

METHOD

Sift the flour for the pastry into a large bowl and add the salt and sugar. Cut the cold butter into cubes and rub into the flour with your fingers until the mixture resembles breadcrumbs. Add the egg yolk (reserving the white) and just enough of the water to bring the mixture together into a ball. We like it as short as possible, so don't worry if it's a little crumbly and hard to handle. Shape into a thick disc, cover in cling film and put in the fridge for 30 to 40 minutes.

Preheat the oven to 180°C fan/gas 6.

Roll out your chilled pastry on a lightly floured surface into a 5mm-thick round. Flip this on to a 25cm loose-bottomed tart tin, patching any pieces that have crumbled or torn. You want to make the walls of the pastry come slightly over the side of the tart tin.

Line the pastry case with baking parchment, fill with baking beans and place in the oven for 20 minutes. Remove from the oven, lift out the paper and beans, prick the base with a fork and return to the oven for 10 minutes, until golden. Let the pie case cool in its tin for 3 minutes on a rack, then brush with the reserved egg white. Remove the pie case from the tin and place on a plate.

Continued on page 191

Family farm run by
Ros

- 600g blueberries
- 120ml water, plus an extra
  2 tablespoons
- 2 tablespoons corn starch
- 100g caster sugar
- 1 tablespoon lemon juice

a pinch of sea salt

FOR THE LEMON
CURD CREAM:

- 50g butter
- 110g caster sugar
- grated zest and juice
  of 2 lemons
- 2 medium eggs and
  1 egg yolk, beaten
- 110g mascarpone cheese
- 2 tablespoons icing sugar

To make the filling, put 150g of the blueberries in a saucepan with 120ml of water, cover and bring to the boil. Meanwhile, in a small bowl, whisk together the corn starch and about 2 tablespoons of water.

When the blueberries and water have come to the boil, lower the heat to a simmer, stirring constantly until the blueberries start to burst and the juices begin to thicken. Add the corn starch mixture, caster sugar, lemon juice and salt. Simmer for 1 minute until the mixture becomes translucent. Remove from the heat and stir in the remaining blueberries.

Spoon the mixture into the pie case and allow to sit for 2 hours.

To make the lemon curd cream, melt the butter in a small saucepan over a very low heat. Add the caster sugar, lemon zest and juice, then add the beaten eggs. Stir carefully with a straight-ended wooden spatula until the mixture coats the back of it. Remove from the heat and allow to cool.

Put the mascarpone into a bowl, add the lemon curd, sift over the icing sugar and gently mix together. You can spoon this mixture on top of the pie or serve it on the side.

Flourless Dark Chocolate and Sea Salt Cake

This is an incredibly rich, salty-sweet chocolate cake that's perfect for dessert. The egg whites provide just enough rise and lightness. The darkness of the chocolate is up to you. We've gone for 70 per cent here, as any higher will make your cake a little bitter. The combination of rich dark chocolate and salt manages to be both sophisticated and sweet – delicious and chic!

MAKES 8 SLICES

- 170g butter, plus extra for greasing
- 350g dark chocolate
- 150g caster sugar
- 5 medium organic eggs
- 50g ground almonds
- 2 teaspoons sea salt, plus extra for decoration
- edible gold dust (optional)
- whipped cream, to serve

METHOD

Preheat the oven to 160°C fan/gas 4. Grease a 23cm springform cake tin and line with baking parchment.

Put the butter, the chocolate and the sugar into a large glass bowl over a pan of barely simmering water until the chocolate and butter melt. Be careful not to overheat the mixture. Leave this to cool while you separate the eggs.

Add the egg yolks to the bowl one at a time, beating into the mixture as you go. Whisk the egg whites into stiff peaks in a separate bowl.

Fold the ground almonds into the chocolate along with the sea salt and half of the whisked egg whites. Carefully incorporate the rest of the egg whites, folding them through the mixture.

Transfer the mix into the prepared cake tin and bake in the oven for 30 to 40 minutes. The top should be well set, with cracks around the circumference so the middle seems to be breaking away from the sides. Leave to cool for at least 15 minutes, then transfer to a plate and decorate with large flakes of sea salt (or edible gold dust, as we like to). Serve with big dollops of softly whipped cream.

Lemon and Lavender Cake

Lavender in cooking poses a bit of a problem: how do you capture that background flavour and aroma – the one that transports you to a summer's day in Provence – without it tasting like soap? Some people recommend staying away from dried lavender and sticking to products like lavender extract paste. However, this is hard to find. Dried lavender works wonderfully, as long as you grind it up so that people aren't biting into whole buds! Combining lavender with lemon and yoghurt makes this cake sticky, subtle and utterly delicious.

MAKES 8–10 SLICES

- butter, for greasing
- 1 tablespoon dried lavender flowers
- 250g caster sugar
- 175g cream flour
- ½ teaspoon baking powder
- ½ teaspoon bicarbonate of soda
- a pinch of sea salt
- 2 medium organic eggs
- 250g Greek yoghurt
- 125ml rapeseed oil
- finely grated zest and juice of 1 lemon
- dried lavender sprigs, to decorate

FOR THE ICING:

- 200g icing sugar
- juice of 1 lemon
- 1 medium egg white

METHOD

Preheat the oven to 160°C fan/gas 4. Butter a 20cm springform cake tin and line with baking parchment.

Crush the lavender in a pestle and mortar. Put the caster sugar into a large bowl and mix the lavender through. Add the flour, baking powder, bicarbonate of soda and salt, and stir to combine.

In another bowl, mix the eggs with the yoghurt and rapeseed oil and pour this into the dry ingredients, stirring well. Add the lemon zest and juice.

Pour the mixture into the cake tin and bake in the oven for around 50 minutes until golden brown and firm to the touch. Leave to cool in the tin for a minute, then turn the cake out to cool fully on a wire rack.

Sieve the icing sugar into a bowl and add the lemon juice, whisking until smooth. Add the egg white gradually to loosen the mixture until it is quite runny and pourable. The icing should be extremely sharp and lemony. Spoon this icing over the top of the cake until it covers the top and starts to drip down the sides.

Arrange some dried lavender sprigs on the top as decoration.

Soaked Orange Cake

Come hail, rain or shine, this cake will always be sitting on the kitchen table of William's mother, Breda, in Currabinny. It is perpetually being baked, eaten and replaced. This cake just says 'home'. It is always moist, and the flavour is even more orangey the next day. William likes to add Campari for a deeper orange flavour, but the original recipe leaves it out.

MAKES 8–10 SLICES

- butter, for greasing
- 50g breadcrumbs (made from slightly stale bread)
- 200g caster sugar
- 110g ground almonds
- 2 teaspoons baking powder
- zest of 1 orange
- zest of 1 lemon
- 4 medium organic eggs
- 200ml rapeseed oil
- candied orange peel (optional), to decorate

FOR THE SYRUP:

- juice of 1 large orange
- juice of 1 lemon
- 50ml Campari or Aperol
- 70g caster sugar
- 1 cinnamon stick

METHOD

Butter and line a 20cm springform cake tin. In a large bowl, combine the breadcrumbs, caster sugar, ground almonds, baking powder and orange and lemon zests.

In a jug, whisk the eggs with the oil and pour into the bowl of dry ingredients, then stir well to combine.

Pour into your prepared tin and place in a cold oven. Turn the oven to 170°C fan/gas 5 and bake for 45 to 60 minutes. You want the cake to be firm, golden brown and definitely not soggy in the middle. If the cake is browning too quickly, cover it with some tinfoil or even turn the oven down a little. You'll know the cake is done when a skewer comes out clean.

While the cake is baking, make the syrup. Heat the ingredients in a pan over a medium heat until gently simmering, then turn the heat down to low and simmer for 5 minutes.

When the cake is ready, leave in the tin, pierce all over with a fork and pour the syrup over the cake until it has been soaked up, reserving the cinnamon stick.

When the cake has cooled completely, release it from the tin and decorate with the cinnamon stick or some candied orange peel.

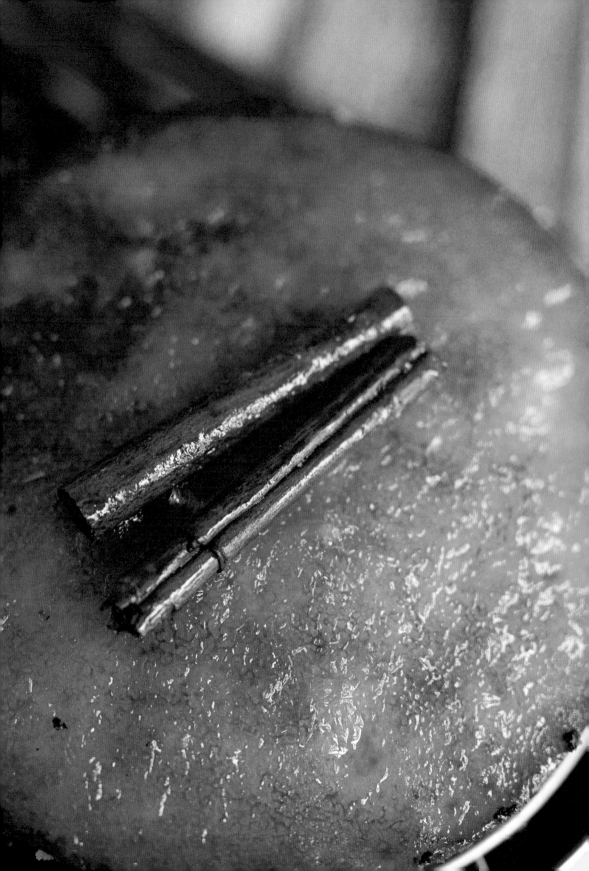

Wholemeal Spelt Carrot Loaf with Orange Mascarpone Icing

This manages to be both indulgent and really healthy (well, as healthy as any cake gets!). The recipe includes wholemeal spelt flour, which gives the loaf a moreish nuttiness.

MAKES 8 SLICES

- 75ml rapeseed oil, plus extra for greasing
- 175g carrots
- 2 medium organic eggs
- 110g soft brown sugar
- 100g wholemeal spelt flour
- 1 teaspoon baking powder
- 1½ teaspoons bicarbonate of soda
- 50g desiccated coconut
- 1 teaspoon ground cinnamon
- ½ teaspoon ground nutmeg

FOR THE ICING:

- 250g mascarpone cheese
- 2 tablespoons icing sugar
- juice of 1 orange
- a few chopped walnuts (for decoration)
- some orange zest (for decoration – use as much as you like)

METHOD

Preheat the oven to 190°C fan/gas 6. Grease and line a 450g loaf tin with baking parchment.

Peel the carrots and grate them finely. In a large bowl, whisk the eggs and brown sugar until thick and creamy. Continuing to whisk, slowly pour the oil into the egg mixture until well combined.

In another bowl, gently mix the flour, baking powder, bicarbonate of soda, coconut, cinnamon and nutmeg together. Add to the batter in three batches, folding in well each time, then add the grated carrots, stirring gently to combine. Pour into the lined loaf tin and bake in the oven for 25 minutes.

Meanwhile, put the ingredients for the icing into a bowl and mix well. Use a skewer to test if the loaf is done. When it comes out clean, remove the loaf from the oven and cool on a wire rack. Once cooled, use a spatula to cover the loaf with icing and sprinkle over some chopped walnuts and some orange zest if you like.

Pecan and White Chocolate Banana Loaf

If someone is coming over to the house for catch-ups, this is our go-to recipe. We can whip it up in no time, and a few slices go down a treat with a pot of tea. Also, it's full of bananas, so it's one of your five-a-day! If you can get your hands on some dried flower petals, sprinkle them over the top once it's done to get extra marks for effort.

MAKES 8 SLICES

- 125g butter, plus 1 tablespoon for the tin
- 175g cream flour, plus extra for dusting
- 4 small, ripe bananas
- 100g white chocolate
- 60g pecans
- 2 teaspoons baking powder
- ½ teaspoon bicarbonate of soda
- ½ teaspoon sea salt
- 150g caster sugar
- 2 medium organic eggs
- 1 teaspoon vanilla extract

METHOD

Preheat the oven to 160°C fan/gas 4. Melt all the butter in a small saucepan on a low heat. Brush the inside of a 900g loaf tin with 1 tablespoon of the butter, then dust with flour.

Mash the bananas, chop the white chocolate into chunks and roughly chop the pecans. Mix the flour with the baking powder, bicarbonate of soda and salt in a bowl.

In a separate, large bowl, whisk the rest of the melted butter and sugar together. Beat in the eggs, one at a time, then stir in the mashed bananas, white chocolate chunks, pecans and vanilla extract.

Add the dry ingredients to the wet ingredients in three batches, stirring after each addition. Pour into the loaf tin and bake in the oven for 1 to 1¼ hours, or until a skewer comes out clean. Slide a spatula around the edge of the loaf and leave in the tin to cool before turning out on to a wire rack.

Now, devour.

Glamnilla Shortbread Biscuits

We love sitting at home in the evening, watching documentaries with a pot of tea and a big plate of vanilla shortbread biscuits. To add a bit of glamour when we sold them at our first market stall, we coated them with some edible gold dust, and they looked so gorgeous that James Snapchatted them. One of his followers said they should be called 'Glamnillas' – and that was that! If you've friends over for tea, arrange some on a white plate: you'll be totally channelling Marie Antoinette.

MAKES 20

- 170g cream flour, plus extra for dusting
- 1 vanilla pod
- 110g cold butter
- 55g caster sugar
- edible gold dust, to finish (optional)

METHOD

Put the flour into a chilled bowl. Slice open the vanilla pod lengthways, and with the back of a knife scrape the seeds out of the pod and add the seeds to the flour. Cut the butter into small chunks and add to the flour, along with the sugar. Rub together with your fingers until the mixture starts to come together. The idea is to create a very short, crumbly dough with very little moisture.

Pat the dough into a flat disc, cover in cling film and chill for 15 minutes in the fridge. Preheat the oven to 160°C fan/gas 4.

Roll out the dough on a lightly floured surface to about 3mm thick (i.e. quite thin). Cut out shapes with pastry cutter/s of your choice; we like to keep things as simple as possible with a small round one.

Arrange on a baking tray lined with baking parchment, leaving around 1cm between each biscuit to allow for expansion. Gather up the trimmings, roll out and cut your shapes out again until you've used up all the dough.

Bake in the oven for 10 to 15 minutes, until the biscuits are a very light golden colour. Keep a watchful eye on them, as they will brown very quickly. When ready, immediately remove from the baking tray and arrange on a cooling rack. Dust lightly with edible gold dust for an extra-special touch. They will keep for a couple of days in an airtight jar or tin in a cool place.

Rock Sugar Biscuits

Making these lovely-looking textured biscuits is simple and a real treat – there's nothing like doing a bit of bashing with a rolling pin to get rid of stress!

MAKES 10–15

- 180g butter, softened
- 140g caster sugar
- 2 medium egg whites
- 1 tablespoon mixed spice
- 1 teaspoon sea salt
- 300g cream flour
- 150g white sugar cubes

METHOD

Cream the butter, caster sugar and half the egg whites with the mixed spice and salt until smooth and pale. Sift the flour into the mixture in three batches, beating it in each time with a wooden spoon until well incorporated and a dough has formed. Shape the dough into a disc, wrap in cling film and refrigerate for half an hour.

Wrap the sugar cubes in a clean tea towel and beat with a rolling pin until they're all broken up into individual grains.

Preheat the oven to 150°C fan/gas 3.

Roll the dough out on to a large piece of baking parchment into a 3mm-thick, roughly square shape. Brush the dough with the remaining egg white and sprinkle the sugar granules over it. Score the surface of the dough into biscuit-sized squares, making sure you don't cut all the way through.

Lift the parchment carefully on to a baking tray and bake in the oven for 30 to 40 minutes. Remove from the oven when golden and leave to cool on the parchment. When cool you can break along the pre-cuts into their individual squares. They will keep for a couple of days in an airtight jar or tin in a cool place.

Molasses Biscuits

The rich, full-bodied flavour of molasses makes these biscuits the perfect accompaniment to strong coffee.

MAKES AROUND 40

- 180g butter
- 100g molasses
- 180g soft brown sugar
- 280g cream flour
- 1 teaspoon ground cinnamon
- ½ teaspoon ground ginger
- 1 teaspoon bicarbonate of soda
- a pinch of sea salt
- 1 medium organic egg
- 50g rolled oats

METHOD

Preheat the oven to 160°C fan/gas 4. Line two baking trays with baking parchment.

Melt the butter in a large, heavy-based saucepan over a medium heat, then add the molasses and sugar and stir until the sugar has dissolved. Remove from the heat and leave to cool.

In a large bowl, mix the flour, cinnamon, ginger, bicarbonate of soda and salt together.

Whisk the egg into the cooled molasses mixture until smooth, add the oats and stir through. Add the dry mixture to the molasses mixture in batches, stirring to combine into a firm but sticky dough.

Get tablespoons of the dough and roll into balls with your hands. Place on the baking trays about 2½cm apart. Bake in the oven for 10 to 15 minutes until hard and medium brown in colour. After cooling for a few minutes on the trays, transfer to wire racks to cool fully. They will keep for a couple of days in an airtight jar or tin in a cool place.

Lemon and Rosemary Biscuits

Moving from Cork to Dublin, William naturally brought some staples to remind him of home – including Barry's Tea and a big bag of stoneground Macroom Oatmeal. Luckily, James was already a Barry's convert, which made moving in together a lot easier. The oatmeal was a harder sell. James is not one for porridge, and this hardy oatmeal is apparently considered an acquired taste in Dublin. He is, however, a huge fan of biscuits. In this recipe the natural nuttiness and roughness of the oatmeal goes beautifully with the earthy fragrance of rosemary and the sharpness of lemon.

MAKES 20

- 225g butter, softened
- 100g caster sugar
- 1 medium organic egg
- 1 tablespoon lemon zest
- 1 teaspoon vanilla bean paste
- 200g cream flour
- 85g Macroom Oatmeal
- a pinch of sea salt
- 1 tablespoon finely chopped fresh rosemary

METHOD

Cream the butter and sugar together in a large bowl until light and fluffy, then beat the egg in slowly with the lemon zest and vanilla, being careful not to split the mixture. In another bowl, mix the flour, oatmeal, salt and rosemary.

Gently add the dry ingredients to the butter mixture, stirring slowly until well combined into a smooth dough. Shape the dough into two logs and cover in cling film. Freeze the logs for 1 hour.

Preheat the oven to 180°C fan/gas 6.

Remove the logs from the freezer, take off the cling film and slice into rounds 6mm thick. Place on a baking tray lined with baking parchment, leaving 2cm between each biscuit.

Bake in the oven for 15 to 20 minutes until the biscuits are golden around the edges. Cool on the baking tray for a few minutes, then transfer to a wire rack to cool fully. They will keep for a couple of days in an airtight jar or tin in a cool place.

Orange Shortbread with Salted Dark Chocolate

This pairing of orange and dark chocolate is a classic. You can think of these as inspired by Jaffa Cakes – they are like a fancier version!

MAKES 25–30 BISCUITS

- 115g butter, softened
- 65g caster sugar
- 2 teaspoons fresh orange juice
- 130g cream flour
- 2 teaspoons orange zest, plus extra for sprinkling

FOR THE SALTED DARK CHOCOLATE:

- 350g dark chocolate (70%)
- 2 teaspoons sea salt

METHOD

Put the butter and sugar into a large bowl and beat vigorously with a wooden spoon until creamy (you could use a hand-held mixer if you prefer). Add the orange juice slowly, being careful that the mixture does not split.

Sift in the flour, then add the orange zest, working the two ingredients into the butter and sugar mixture until a smooth dough forms. If the dough is too sticky and wet, add a little more flour.

Roll the dough into a sausage shape around 4cm in diameter and wrap in baking parchment. Chill the dough in the freezer for 1 hour.

Preheat the oven to 160°C fan/gas 4. Line two baking sheets with baking parchment.

After the dough has hardened, remove the baking parchment and slice into rounds 3mm thick. Place these rounds on your baking sheets and bake in the oven for 10 to 15 minutes until lightly golden. Transfer to a wire rack, being careful they don't break – they will be quite soft and delicate – and leave to cool until crisp and hard.

While your shortbread is cooling, melt the dark chocolate in a heatproof bowl over a pan of gently simmering water. Keep stirring the chocolate as it melts. Turn the heat off but leave the bowl over the hot water to keep warm. Stir the salt through the melted chocolate.

When the biscuits have cooled, dip them halfway
into the chocolate, leaving one half bare. Leave
to set on sheets of baking parchment.

Before the chocolate on the biscuits has completely
hardened, sprinkle some orange zest over them.
You can store them for a couple of days in an airtight
jar or tin in a cool place.

Honey Biscuits

These biscuits could not be easier to make. But the inclusion of
beautiful wildflower honey raises their flavour to another level and
makes them really special.

MAKES 50–60

- 300g cream flour
- 1 teaspoon bicarbonate of soda
- a pinch of sea salt
- 240g butter
- 150g caster sugar
- 2 generous tablespoons good honey, such as wildflower or orange blossom

METHOD

Preheat the oven to 160°C fan/gas 4. Line two baking
trays with baking parchment.

Sift the flour and bicarbonate of soda into a large
bowl and add the salt. In a small saucepan, heat the
butter, sugar and honey until the sugar has dissolved.
Remove from the heat and pour into the flour mixture.
Mix together with a fork to form a smooth dough.

Using a teaspoon, place small balls of dough on the
prepared baking trays and press down with the back
of the spoon into thick discs.

Bake in the oven for 10 to 12 minutes until golden. Allow
to cool on the trays for a few minutes, then transfer to a
wire rack to cool completely. They will keep for a couple
of days in an airtight jar or tin in a cool place.

Currabinny Brown Apple Tray Bake

Four gnarled and hardy apple trees grow behind the house at Currabinny. On windy nights the sounds of apples getting blown on to the roof can give people sleeping underneath quite a fright! This simple, soothing, warmly spiced tray bake is a lovely home for the apples that make it through the stormy nights.

SERVES 6-8

- butter, for greasing
- 225g wholemeal self-raising flour
- 25g ground almonds
- 1 teaspoon mixed spice
- 1 teaspoon ground cinnamon
- ½ teaspoon freshly grated nutmeg
- a pinch of sea salt
- 100g brown sugar, plus extra to sprinkle on top
- 100g cold butter
- 400g Bramley apples
- 2 medium organic eggs
- 2 tablespoons milk
- 25g flaked almonds

METHOD

Preheat the oven to 160°C fan/gas 4. Butter a square (25cm x 25cm) deep-sided baking tray or rectangular (24cm x 28cm) casserole dish.

In a large bowl, mix together the flour, ground almonds, mixed spice, cinnamon, nutmeg, salt and sugar. Cube the cold butter and add to the bowl, rubbing it into the mixture with your fingertips until it's a fine breadcrumb-like consistency.

Peel and core the apples and chop them into chunks. Beat the eggs in a small bowl with the milk. Add the apple, then the egg mixture to the bowl of dry ingredients, stirring with a wooden spoon as you do it. This will create a soft batter.

Pour the batter into your prepared tray or dish and scatter the flaked almonds and some brown sugar over the top. Bake in the oven for 40 to 45 minutes until risen and firm to the touch – the colour should be dark brown but watch out for burning at the edges. Remove from the oven and leave to cool before cutting into squares.

Patrick O'Hara's Elderflower Cordial

WILLIAM'S NEIGHBOUR IN CURRABINNY,
ARTIST PATRICK O'HARA, MAKES A
GORGEOUS ELDERFLOWER CORDIAL EVERY
SUMMER. HERE PATRICK KINDLY SHARES HIS
TOP TIPS AND RECIPE SO THAT YOU CAN
MAKE THIS REFRESHING DRINK YOURSELF.

At the tip of the Currabinny peninsula there is a 90-acre forested sugarloaf hill which is topped by an ancient stone circle and cairn – reputed to be a focal point of magical and strange happenings. Around its edges are some of our more exotic shrubs and bushes, thriving in the balmy microclimate created by the Gulf Stream, which washes around the shoreline. Among them are some of the finest examples of our native Irish elder shrubs.

Elder reaches its peak flowering time around 21 June – Midsummer's Day – and its flowers can produce one of the most delicious and refreshing soft drinks. Elder branches are brittle and easily broken, so you must be careful when you pick the **40 or so umbrella-shaped heads of creamy white flowers** needed for this recipe. They are best gathered on a hot, dry, sunny day, as close as possible to midday, when the tiny flowers are newly opened and giving off maximum fragrance.

Put them into a clean plastic bucket with a lid and add **about 3 litres of boiling water, a couple of roughly chopped oranges and lemons, about 1½ kilos of granulated or caster sugar and an 85g sachet of citric acid.**

Continued on page 215

Cover and leave for 48 hours. Then stir daily for 10–14 days with a potato masher, with which you can also gently squash the citrus fruit. After this time, leave it unstirred for a day before pouring it all through a large, coarse sieve into a sterilized bowl.

Next, pour that cloudy liquid through a jelly-bag or very fine sieve into a sterilized jug, before decanting it into clean, sterilized bottles (preferably the kind with stoppers). You can sterilize glass bottles by washing them in warm, soapy water, rinsing in boiling water, then placing to dry in a preheated oven at 120°C fan/gas 1 for 15 minutes. When you've filled your bottles with cordial, seal immediately.

The cordial is best served with ice and diluted in the ratio of about 1 part cordial and 5 parts sparkling spring water.

Keep in a cool, dark place and it could last for up to 9 months, but it won't – your friends and family will have drunk it all long before that!

I have heard it said that it makes quite a stimulating aftershave as well!

SETTING THE SCENE

Because you – and your guests – are worth it . . .

....

WHETHER SETTING THE TABLE FOR ONE,
TWO OR EIGHT PEOPLE, IT ALWAYS LIFTS
THE MOOD AND SOMEHOW MAKES YOUR
FOOD TASTE EVEN BETTER IF YOU MAKE
AN EFFORT WITH YOUR SURROUNDINGS.

....

We are big fans of vintage shops for sourcing unusual and attractive cups, plates, bowls, sauce boats, platters and all kinds of intriguing tableware to showcase our food.

When it comes to cutlery, we like the warmth and softness of bronze, coppers and muted silvers (we like to support Irish companies and are delighted we can get great cutlery from Newbridge Silverware). We love to use tablecloths and cloth napkins, and we find that natural colours look best – greys, browns and beige tend to work well in any situation (again, we try to go local for dressing our table and we get lovely table linen from STABLE of Ireland).

Candlelight is the best light. Candelabras and candlesticks look gorgeous – often far more impressive than they cost. Again, you'll get great ones with a lovely weathered look in vintage shops. Add them to your dining armoury to pull out for special occasions. Place them along the centre of the table and everyone will be bathed in a glow of soft golden light.

No table setting is complete without flowers. We love purples, whites and greens, things like flowering cabbage, baby's breath, thistle and hydrangea. We like our flowers to look as if they have been picked from an overgrown country garden. Uniformity when it comes to flowers isn't a good look!

Now, this may sound a bit over the top, but never underestimate the value of a place card when you have people over. Even if you're just having a few friends around for a casual dinner, taking a bit of extra time to write their names on cards will create a lovely talking point (and some nice social media content for guests who are sharing your dinner with their followers!).

Depending on the occasion you can customize your place cards, or come up with simple but ingenious card-holders; for example, when the colder months come around, pine cones add a beautiful seasonal touch to the table.

NEVER UNDERESTIMATE THE VALUE OF A PLACE CARD WHEN YOU HAVE PEOPLE OVER

Another great benefit of place cards is social engineering! You may be entertaining people who don't know each other well, or who you know will chat more easily with one guest than another; using place cards allows you to orchestrate the atmosphere around the table.

Those are our tips for setting the scene for a simple and memorable meal. But the main thing to do is relax. Plan to serve something that you're happy making and something you can prepare in advance. And if something goes wrong, don't panic; just pass around some nice bread and toppings and fill up everyone's glasses. Sláinte!

Thanks . . .

To everyone below – we could not have written our first cookbook without you!

First, to our parents – Gags and Alan, Breda and Peter – for all the lifts and the general support, both moral and practical, you've given us. Special thanks to Gags and Breda for the recipes you shared with us, for your advice, and for cooking your signature dishes for the book. And thanks to Breda and Peter for letting us take over the house in Currabinny for the shoot.

To our neighbours in Phibsboro – Bang Bang Café and the Vintage Shop – for allowing us to take pictures in the café and shop for the book. Thanks to Daniel and Grace in Bang Bang for feeding us your delicious Brunch Burgers and to the Vintage for having the coolest dinnerware.

Thanks also to all the stallholders at the Mahon Point Farmers' Market for your wonderful produce and being so game for being photographed for the book. A special thanks to Patrick O'Hara of Currabinny for sharing your elderflower cordial recipe and agreeing to have your picture included.

To everyone who worked on the shoot: Bríd O'Donovan for taking the most delicious photographs; Jette Virdi for your flawless food-styling skills; Ciara Nolan – no one chops vegetables quite like you; and Aoife Datta for your great help in the kitchen. And thanks to Andrew McLaughlin, who took some great shots and footage during the making of this book and is a whizz on social media.

Also, to those who supplied wonderful props and produce for the shoot: Helen James for the beautiful plates and crockery; STABLE of Ireland for the lovely fabrics that helped set the scene in many of our photographs; Lynn Hunter for the plates (that we still need to return to you – sorry!); and Nudie Foods for all the lovely fruit and vegetables.

Thanks to Susan McKeever and Caroline Pretty for getting the text into such good shape. And to Danielle O'Connell for your gorgeous work designing the book and for helping bring our vision to life.

Thanks to Penguin Ireland for believing in us – to our editor, Patricia Deevy; to Michael McLoughlin, MD; to Cliona Lewis, Aimée Johnston and Aislin Reddie on the publicity team; and to Carrie Anderson and Brian Walker in sales. And in London thanks to Sara Granger, Natalie Wall and Emma Brown, who made sure the book stayed on track in the production process.

Thanks to our housemate Edel, who heard a lot about this project over the last couple of years – you've been very patient! William wants to specially thank Lorra Kent, his manager at l'Gueuleton, and also his colleagues there for all the support – for time off to work on the book and for putting up with him when he was getting stressed about it!

Thanks to Darina, Rory, Rachel and the teachers at Ballymaloe, who helped to instil in us a great food ethos. Ballymaloe is the spiritual home of Irish food and we are honoured to have been able to spend time with the great team there, and to return frequently – you constantly inspire us. Thanks also to Blathnaid Bergin for your superb advice on the business of food.

To all the people who have contributed to our food journey from childhood onwards. To William's 'second parents', Pat 'the potter' Cunningham and Ann O'Regan, for your passion for food, learning and sharing. To all the people who have helped us at the markets, events and suppers that have brought us to this point: Anna Moloney, Ciaran Murphy, Igor Brodecki, Joy Freeman, Silvio Barletti, Shaylyn Gilheaney, Anna Burke, Kyle Cheldon Barnett, Lynda Burke, Kate Mcelroy, Mark Geraghty, Jill and Gill and so many more. You have encouraged us, been generous with your knowledge and advice, and shaped the approach to food that we share in this book. We look forward to continuing the journey alongside all of you.

Finally, a massive thanks to our Currabinny followers – sure, we wouldn't be able to do this if you didn't like our food!

INDEX

P

PENGUIN IRELAND

UK | USA | CANADA | IRELAND | AUSTRALIA

INDIA | NEW ZEALAND | SOUTH AFRICA

Penguin Ireland is part of the Penguin Random House group of companies
whose addresses can be found at global.penguinrandomhouse.com.

Penguin
Random House
UK

First published 2018
001

Colour reproduction by Altaimage Ltd
Printed in China

A CIP catalogue record for this book is available from the British Library

ISBN: 978–1–844–88414–8

www.greenpenguin.co.uk